CORVETTE
ROADSTER

Contents

ISBN: 0-517-61045-0

BEEKMAN HOUSE
Distributed by Crown Publishers, Inc.
225 Park Avenue South
New York, New York 10003

Printed and bound by
Grafički zavod Hrvatske, Zagreb, Yugoslavia
10 9 8 7 6 5 4 3 2 1

Photo credits
Photography was supplied by General Motors Corporation and Chevrolet Division except as follows: Jim Dunne (page 43), Roland Flessner (pages 48-50), David Gooley (page 15), Richard D. Hawthorne (page 63), Bert Johnson (page 36), Bud Juneau (pages 18-20), Doug Mitchel (pages 23-24, 25, 26, 30-31), Nicky Wright (pages 10-11).

Introduction

The joy of driving automobiles emerges from their capacity to allow us enjoyment through all of our senses. That is what endears them to so many people. Automakers who understand the impact of quality sensory input will establish a significant, long-lasting reputation with enthusiasts. Of all the different types of automobiles that have been built through the years, the most sensory-packed are

First 'Vette roadster since '75.

those with open tops. Whether they're called convertibles, roadsters, cabriolets, or spyders, they provide open-air driving that sharpens the sensory perceptions of their drivers and passengers.

In the early Fifties, Chevrolet started a tradition in motoring that now carries over into today—the company built the Corvette roadster, an American sports car meant to appeal to the enthusiasts bitten by the European sports car bug in the Forties. But the Corvette wasn't like the European cars; instead, it paved its own way into the hearts of supporters in the

United States and across the ocean, not
relying on past criteria but creating its own
as the years passed. Body materials, styling,
and drivetrain set apart the Corvettes,
which continued as roadsters along with
the newer coupes into their fifth
generation.

The Corvette roadster bowed out after
the 1975 model year, the victim of
increased emphasis on safety and
threatened legislation. It has been sorely
missed, leaving a gap in Chevrolet's sports
car lineup. For ten years, that gap
remained unfilled except by a few custom

Roadster—open top and 230 bhp.

houses that would attempt to modify the Corvette body.

With the advent of the sixth-generation Corvette in 1984, roadsters still weren't in sight. After two more years of speculation, the public has been treated to the intro-duction of the best Corvette roadster yet for the 1986 model year. It will satisfy those who want to experience motoring with all of their senses. As an added bonus, it is the pace car for the 1986 Indianapolis 500.

Welcome back, Corvette roadster! We've missed you!

Fifties Sports Car:
Initial Concepts for the Corvette

When the first Corvette rolled off the assembly line on June 30, 1953, it started a love affair with the American public that has continued for three and a half decades. While a number of the Corvette's features have been maintained from the first roadster to the current model year—fiberglass bodies, two-passenger seating, the most contemporary engine offerings—dramatic changes have taken place since its introduction. The model has gone through six different styling generations, beginning with the first in 1953. That first production vehicle represented several years of thought and months of frantic planning. If the Corvette could be said to have parents, they would have to be Harley Earl and Ed Cole.

Harley J. Earl was a key figure in the high success enjoyed by General Motors during the late Forties and early Fifties. He founded and headed the firm's Art & Colour Section, the industry's first in-house styling department. Earl seemed to be born to the trade of automotive design. His father had designed horse-drawn carriages in Los Angeles. Young Harley was a devotee of the automobile by the time he was out of Stanford. In the early Twenties, he won fame as the designer of dashing custom bodies for Don Lee, then a leader in the field of Hollywood coachbuilders. At Lee's, Harley Earl was "discovered" by Lawrence P. Fisher of Cadillac. Fisher recommended Earl to General Motors president Alfred P.

Sloan, Jr., and Harley signed aboard at the age of 32.

Earl not only loved cars, but also was very imaginative, and he had the good sense to surround himself with equally talented assistants for whom he provided the most stimulating and creative work environment possible, and many stylists owed their careers to him. Virgil Exner, later to win fame with the "Forward Look" Chrysler products, trained under Earl and headed the Pontiac studio in the Thirties. Frank Hershey, Art Ross, Ned Nickles, and Bill Mitchell made their own marks at Cadillac and Buick. Clare MacKichan, father of the '55 Chevy design, was an Earl trainee. Mitchell went on to become Earl's successor, and had an equally outstanding career.

Harley Earl had almost single-handedly "invented" the dream car with his predictive Buick Y-Job—a long, low, two-seat convertible first displayed in 1938. The car not only set the design themes for the company's styling in the immediate prewar and postwar years, but it also proved the value of giving the public a "sneak preview" of things to come. Such previews led, in turn, to the Motoramas—exciting extravaganzas that thrilled visitors in cities and towns all over the country between 1949 and 1961. Earl's imagination was tempered by a shrewd understanding of public taste, honed at countless Motoramas and public showings.

Earl was eager to return to experimental projects after World War II. Once the corporation's new 1949–50 models had been wrapped up, he did. Significantly, his first postwar dream cars were two-seaters, the aircraft-inspired LeSabre of 1951 and the Buick XP-300 shown a year later. Both featured ideas advanced for the day, including wraparound wind-shields, folding tops hidden just behind the cockpit under metal covers, sculptured rear decks with prominent tail fins, and low, ground-hugging stance.

But Harley Earl had something else on his mind. Karl Ludvigsen writes: "As an antidote to post-LeSabre creative depression, Earl began thinking seriously about a low-priced sporty car during the late fall of 1951. He'd do this in his office on the 11th floor of the anonymous-looking brick structure on the south side of Milwaukee Avenue, opposite the imposing GM Building. Then he'd wander . . . down to the ninth floor. There, in a small enclosure adjacent to the main Body Development Studio, Earl could work privately with a personal crew on projects . . . that he wanted to shield from pre-mature exposure. Earl was well aware of the perishable quality of a new idea." That new idea was the genesis of the Corvette.

The first sketches and scale models for Earl's pet project were, as Ludvigsen describes, "most like an amalgam of the classic British sports cars and the [Willys] Jeepster, for Earl had in mind a very simple car, one that could be priced at only $1850—about as much as a Ford, Chevy, or Studebaker sedan in 1952. A price this moderate meant that the design had to be based on a more or less stock chassis, and that's the way the first tentative studies went." New inspiration came from a car displayed for a time in GM's Styling Auditorium. Called "Alembic I," it was essentially the original Bill Tritt design for U.S. Rubber Company, which had purchased it and loaned it to GM. Earl now stepped up the pace, and work proceeded as "Project Opel"—a name perhaps chosen to confuse outsiders, although Chevrolet frequently did advanced studies for GM's German subsidiary in those days. The work was all very secret, with access limited only to those who had a "need to know." If an employee wasn't directly involved with the "Opel" program, chances are that he would never have heard about it.

At about that time, Edward N. Cole was transferred from Cadillac Division to Chevrolet, where he took over as chief engineer. Cole would be another key figure in Corvette history, but his list of credits was already impressive. He had come to Cadillac in 1933 after taking part in a work-study program at the GM Institute. His first assignments involved designing military vehicles such as light tanks for the Army. After the war he worked on rear-engine prototypes for both Cadillac and Chevrolet; then he concentrated on engines, helping Cadillac's John Gordon to develop that division's short-stroke

The 1954 Corvettes had the Chevy Blue Flame in-line six-cylinder engine for a powerplant. Where the '53 line came in any color as long as it was Polo White, the '54's were also available in Pennant Blue and Sportsman Red.

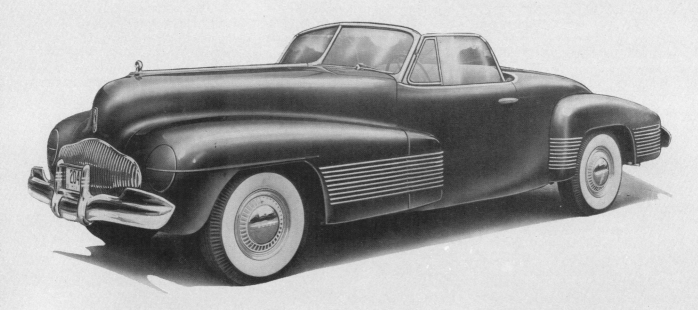

overhead-valve V-8 for 1949. Cole then managed Cadillac's Cleveland plant for 30 months before taking his new job at Chevy. Once installed, he more than doubled the engineering staff—from 850 to 2900—then turned to designing a new V-8 for Chevrolet. That new engine was the legendary small-block 265-cubic-inch unit introduced in 1955.

In Art & Colour, Earl had tapped Robert F. McLean, a young sports car enthusiast with degrees from Cal Tech in both engineering and industrial design, to come up with a basic layout for Project Opel. Though assured that he couldn't, McLean started his design from the back, not the front as was the usual practice. With the rear axle as a reference point, he placed the passenger and engine compartments as close to it as possible, the goal being the balanced 50/50 weight distribution

desirable in a sports car for optimum handling. The actual figure worked out to be 53/47 percent front and rear, still a credible figure. Wheelbase was pegged at 102 inches, the same as that of the Jaguar XK-120, one of Harley Earl's favorite cars. Track dimensions would be 57 inches front and 59 inches rear, wider than the Jaguar's but not as wide proportionally as on the new rear-engine Porsches.

Styling work was by now being coordinated with the engineering effort, and Earl's staff began incorporating ideas from his LeSabre and XP-300 show cars into the body for Project Opel. So far, Earl's sports car was still only a proposal—a dream car for the Motorama, maybe, but a long way from production. Yet, as Ludvigsen notes, Earl "envisioned new popularity for sports car racing throughout America with [his] car

readily available, saying expansively that people would soon forget about those English cars as soon as these sporty Chevys were on the market." Not surprisingly, and with examples like the "Alembic I" at hand, he looked to fiberglass as the best means for holding the line on body tooling expenses. As for the chassis, McLean's layout would somehow have to be realized with existing Chevy hardware, some of which might be modified to suit the new platform. No other choice was available.

But the use of fiberglass presented two big unanswered questions: Would it provide the requisite body strength? How would it work in actual production? The second question could not be answered without a production go-ahead, of course, but the first question was answered dramatically in an "accidental" fashion. Chevy had built a full-size

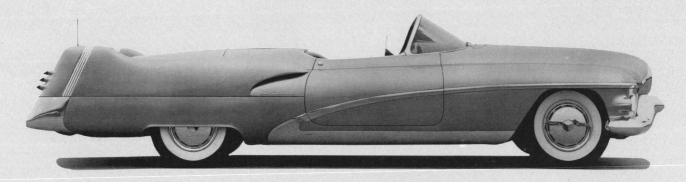

Harley Earl's show cars affected the eventual design of the Corvette. Opposite page, top: The Buick Y-Job was first displayed in 1938. Bottom: The LeSabre show car had a cover over the folded top. Above: A '54 'Vette with the three '54 Motorama cars, including the Nomad wagon and the Corvair fastback.

convertible with a fiberglass-reinforced plastic body strictly for investigative research and development purposes in early 1952. During high-speed testing at the proving grounds, the test driver accidently rolled the car, emerging unhurt. Amazingly, the car's body suffered no severe damage. Now Earl was more convinced than ever that fiberglass was the way to go.

By mid-1952, the basic outlines of the new sports car had been laid down, Ed Cole was abroad as Chevrolet's new engineering chief, and Harley Earl was working toward completion of the two-seat car in time for the 1953 Motorama. Cole became one of the first people within Chevy Division to see what Earl was doing. Ludvigsen records that, according to one witness at the showing, Cole "literally jumped up and down" and promised to support Earl in his efforts to win production approval all the way to the 14th floor of GM headquarters.

Only one thing remained to be done: a preselling job on General Motors president Harlow Curtice. A few weeks after Cole had seen the full-size plaster model, Earl set it up in the Styling Auditorium to show his boss and Chevy Division general manager Thomas H. Keating. The curtain flew up with a flourish. Then Earl led the two men around the car, explaining enthusi-

astically that here was not only a profitable new product, but a car that would add much-needed sparkle to the Chevy line. His persuasiveness worked. They agreed to show the car at the first Motorama of 1953, scheduled for the grand ballroom of New York's Waldorf-Astoria Hotel the following January. In the meantime, engineering work with a view to eventual production would proceed as Project EX-122, with the final approval or disapproval to be based largely on show-goers' reactions.

An unusual name—Corvette—was found on the nose and tail of a low, gleaming white roadster at the first Motorama of 1953. Reporters got a sneak preview of GM's latest "dream car" on January 16th, the day before the official opening. In a press release, Myron Scott of Chevrolet's public relations staff explained that a corvette was a type of small, agile, 19th-century warship, and that lately the term had been applied to describe small convoy vessels and subchasers in World War II.

Top General Motors officials were on hand, and they anxiously awaited the reactions of those who streamed into the Waldorf-Astoria to look at the two-seater. In the weeks leading up to the first showing, Harley Earl's sports car

had created excitement within Chevrolet Division. Production engineering was proceeding at full steam, and hopes were high that the public would like the car enough to buy many copies.

An estimated four million people saw the Motorama Corvette, and their response was overwhelmingly positive. Even so, it's clear from drawings and dates that those most responsible for the Corvette—Harley Earl and Ed Cole—never doubted that the car would see production. Certainly there was no objection from Chevrolet general manager Thomas Keating or GM president Harlow Curtice. Production would commence at the earliest possible date, and the new sports car would be available from neighborhood Chevy dealers soon. Harley Earl was delighted. The Corvette was on its way.

Below: Chevrolet staged Corvette parades so the public could see production cars. Opposite page, top: Corvette assembly was moved to St. Louis for model year '54. Bottom: A 1955 V-8 Corvette—note the gold V in the side emblem.

1953–55:
The First-Generation Roadster

1953

Work on the production Corvette began in mid-June of 1952, when long-time Chevrolet suspension engineer Maurice Olley sketched a chassis for Project Opel that was quite close to the eventual production design. His main challenge—and success—was in getting a collection of off-the-shelf Chevy parts to fit under Harley Earl's tightly drawn body. While many of the mechanical modifications made for the first Corvette were aimed toward performance, packaging actually dictated most of them.

The Corvette's suspension was of Chevy design and boringly conventional, but spring rates, shock settings, and ride stabilizer were all calibrated to suit a sporting car. Likewise, the Saginaw steering was a stock General Motors component, but it had a much quicker 16:1 ratio. And the Corvette's steering wheel was an inch smaller in diameter than that of Chevy passenger cars.

The Motorama Corvette was one of the few show cars that went into production with its styling virtually intact. That Art & Colour's original design was retained, unsullied by committee modi-

fications, enhances the appeal of early Corvettes among collectors today. There were dozens of detail differences, of course, between the Motorama car and the production '53. Underhood features eliminated for production included much chromeplating, a shrouded fan, and pancake-type air cleaners. "Corvette" script at front and rear was also deleted.

Features unique to the new sports roadster included its easy-folding, manually operated fabric top, which disappeared into a covered compartment behind the twin bucket seats. Another first was the top's chrome-edged, removable, Plexiglas side curtains with push-pull vent wings. The Motorama car had exterior push-button door handles similar to those of the 1951 experimental Buick LeSabre, but they didn't make production. To open the Corvette's door, you thrust a hand through an open vent wing and slide the interior door release rearward.

The 300 Corvettes built for the 1953 model year were essentially handmade pilot units. Frames were

supplied by a non-GM source, and the engines came from Chevy's engine plant in Tonawanda, New York. Engine power was from the 235-cubic-inch Blue Flame six, then delivering 105 brake horsepower. For the Corvette, however, it was modified by fitting a high-lift long-duration camshaft, hydraulic valve

lifters, and a high-compression head, all of which brought power up considerably. Three Carter-type YH sidedraft carburetors mounted on a special aluminum manifold did the rest. Result: 150 bhp at 4500 rpm. At the time, Chevy didn't have a manual transmission suitable for an engine of such power, so engineers substituted a two-speed Powerglide automatic with revised shift points for more sporty response—a decision that would later prove controversial. The manual transmission was a casualty of the crash engineering effort and the need to use as many stock components as possible, along with cost considerations growing ever more critical as production loomed closer. The main problem was space. The Blue Flame six sat 13 inches farther back in the Corvette than in the standard Chevys, and the existing three-speed manual gearbox would have interfered with the rearmost of the three carbs. So going with the Power-glide automatic was the only choice. One unexpected bonus came out of the use of the automatic transmission: It was easily converted to floorshift operation. Shift points were raised to match the greater power and torque of the Corvette engine, and

the transmission oil cooler was omitted, because tests had shown that it simply wasn't needed due to the sports car's livelier acceleration.

Engineer Olley's reply to the criticism of the automatic: "The answer is that the typical sports car enthusiast, like the 'average man' or the square root of minus one, is an imaginary quantity. Also, as the sports car appeals to a wider and wider section of the public, the center of gravity of this theoretical individual is shifting from the austerity of the pioneer towards the luxury of modern ideas.... There is no need to apologize for the performance of this car with its automatic trans-mission."

The body components—46 separate pieces—were produced by the Molded Fiber Glass Body Company at Ashtabula, Ohio, and were glued together using wooden jigs. The early production cars showed considerable improvisation. The first 25, for example, used stock Bel Air wheel covers. To simplify assembly and parts inventory, all '53s were finished Polo White, with red and white interiors and black tops. All were equipped with 6.70 × 15 whitewall tires, Delco signal-seeking radio, and recir-culating hot water heater. The

Below: The '53 Corvette's body was made up of 46 pieces of fiberglass—advanced material for the time. Opposite page: The fiberglass body rode on the frame that also carried the Blue Flame in-line six-cylinder engine and driveline.

instrument panel included a clock and a 5000-rpm tachometer. The mesh headlight guards and the clear Plexiglas cover that protected the rear license plate were both illegal in some states, so the owner's manual included instruc-tions for their removal.

Rare and desirable today, the 1953 'Vette was considered something less than wonderful when new. Its typical 0-60 mph time was 11 seconds, and top speed was about 105 mph—not bad for 1953, but hardly in keeping with the state of the sports car art even then. The suggested retail price of the Corvette was $3513.

The verdict from those schooled in the European tradition of sports cars was predictable: They didn't

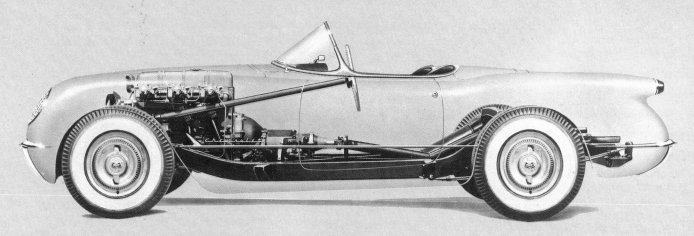

like it. They turned up their noses at the fake knock-off wheel covers, "rocketship" taillights, and the two-speed automatic. Nevertheless, the Corvette was a hit with dealers, who flooded Chevrolet with orders. But the division had decided that the first 300 Corvettes would be reserved mainly for dealers to lend out to local celebrities and prominent business or civic leaders for reaction and evaluation.

1954

For the 1954 model year, Corvette assembly was moved to St. Louis, Missouri, where it would remain until 1981. By the middle of the calendar year, more than 50 cars per day were coming off the assembly line.

Few significant changes were made for the '54s, but running alterations took place through the model year. Tops and top irons were changed from black to tan, and gas and brake lines were relocated inboard of the right-hand main frame rail. The engine carried a newly styled rocker arm cover, the wiring harness was cleaned up, and more plastic-insulated wire replaced the fabric variety. Engines, still built at Flint, were suffixed F54YG. 1954 was also the first year that a choice of colors became available: Pennant Blue metallic (16 percent) with tan interior, Sportsman Red (4 percent) with red and white interior, and the usual Polo White (80 percent) with red interior. A very small number—as few as six—were painted black and carried red interiors. Model year production totalled 3640 units.

The 1953 model had two short stainless steel exhaust extensions, exiting the body inboard of the rear fenders. Owners soon discovered that air turbulence sucked exhaust fumes back against the car, soiling the lacquer. An attempted correction was to lengthen the extensions and to route them out below the body, but that didn't entirely solve the problem. The condition persisted until the new 1956 design, when Corvette chief engineer Zora Arkus-Duntov relocated the exhaust tips to the rear fender extremities.

After about the first 300 units of the 1954 model, the two-handle hood release was replaced with a single-handle unit. At the 1900-unit mark, the three bullet-style air cleaners were dropped in favor of a two-pot type, used through the balance of the model run. A new cam also appeared in later engines, increasing horsepower to 155, a number not revealed until 1955.

The first-generation Corvettes had a few awkward features. To operate the choke, for example, you had to reach across or through the steering wheel with the left hand while operating the ignition with the right hand, because both items were on the right. Subsequently, the choke was moved to the left of the steering column, changing positions with the wiper control. Moisture in the rear license plate compartment caused the plastic lens to fog, so Chevrolet thoughtfully inserted a container with two fabric bags full of a desiccant material to keep the lens clear.

Sales for 1954 proved

disappointing. Even though the Corvette was now available in reasonable quantities from dealers, public response was mixed. Some analysts thought prospective buyers might have viewed it as neither fish nor fowl—not a true road-and-track machine, but not a genuine tourer, either. Purists objected to the automatic transmission and the non-traditional styling. Sporting pleasure drivers didn't like the rude side curtains and manual folding top, and preferred fresh-air heaters to the recirculating unit. Some service problems surfaced, too—water leaks, in particular. Actually, though, real mechanical problems were few. Service bulletins instructed dealers on fixing water leaks, synchronizing the three carburetors, and adjusting for smooth idle—hardly problems of major proportions. The engine, transmission, and driveline were all more than adequate, and they were reliable. However, sales fell and inventories increased. Production slowed, then ground to a halt. At the close of 1954, up to 1500 cars remained unsold. That's amazing in light of the popularity that the 'Vette would later achieve.

1955

Harley Earl had proposed a mild face-lift for 1955, involving a new, wider egg-crate grille similar to that of the '55 Chevrolet passenger models. Budget limitations prevented the face-lift, however, so Corvette remained much as it had been, with one big exception—the new 265-cubic-inch V-8 engine. It was ostensibly an option, but actually no more than 10 six-cylinder Corvettes were built for the entire model year. With the V-8, at last, came the real get-up-and-go that Chevrolet's sports car had needed.

The new V-8 was sensational, producing a rousing 195 brake horsepower at 5000 rpm. It used the conventional passenger-car block and actually weighed about 30 pounds less than the six-cylinder engine. The performance gain was fantastic. It reduced the 0-60 time to between 8.5 and 9.0 seconds, and it raised top speed proportionately, making the Corvette substantially faster than most V-8 sedans of the day. But perhaps more important, the V-8 Corvette was quicker than Ford's Thunderbird. Chevrolet took satisfaction in that.

Shortly after the start of 1955 production, the Pennant Blue color option was replaced by Harvest

Top: Crossed flags on a '55 'Vette hood. Bottom: The interior. Opposite page: Wire mesh covered headlights (Owner: Dave Stefun)

Gold, with contrasting green trim and dark green top, a popular combination. Metallic Corvette Copper was also made available, while Gypsy Red replaced the previous Sportsman Red. The latter came with white vinyl interior and red saddle stitching, tan carpet and top. Aside from color changes, the only exterior modification was a gold V overlaid on the letter V in the Chevrolet side script, to identify the V-8 models.

The 1955 bodies were smoother and slightly thinner in section than before, and workmanship was better. Early production cars display holes in the frame rails for mounting the six-cylinder engine. The underside of the hood X-brace was replaced with a lateral brace in order to clear the V-8's air cleaner. The V-8s also carried an automatic choke for the first time in production. Also, because the new

engine revved higher than the six, the tachometer was changed to a 6000-rpm scale with 500-rpm increments. The electrical system became 12-volt, as on most '55 General Motors cars, although the six-cylinder engine was curiously listed with the six-volt system. V-8s also featured an electric, rather than vacuum-operated, wiper motor, and foot-operated wind-shield washers were reinstated.

The transmission coupled to the V-8 was similar to the previous Powerglide, except that its vacuum modulator was eliminated in keeping with all 1955 Chevrolet production. Kick-down was now governed solely by speed and throttle position. Important trans-mission news, however, came late in the model run, when a small number of cars were built with a new close-ratio three-speed manual

gearbox. The shifter was a small chrome stick, rising from the side of the tunnel and topped by a plain white ball. The boot around the lever was sealed to the floor with a bright metal plate showing the shift pattern. The rear axle ratio was shortened from the usual 3.55:1 Powerglide to 3.70:1.

Unfortunately, 1955 proved to be another sales disappointment. Production totalled only 700 units for the model year. By the end of the Motorama-style car run, quality and performance had been improved considerably, and the option list had been broadened. But the market was still elusive. Ford, meanwhile, was selling 16,155 Thunderbirds—roughly 23 times the volume of Corvette. Again, the Corvette's friends and foes alike asked, "Where do we go from here?" One of the men who helped to answer that question was Zora Arkus-Duntov.

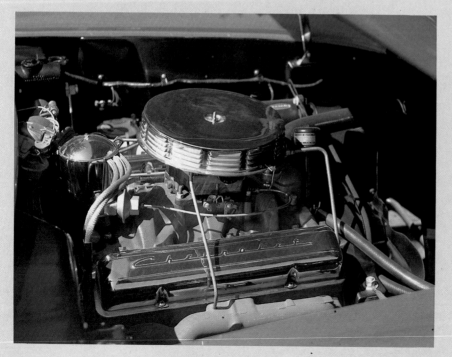

Above: Purists didn't like the first generation taillight wings. Left: The '55's newly introduced V-8 engine finally gave the 'Vette some power. (Owner: Dave Stefun)

1956–57:
The Second-Generation Roadster

1956

The Corvette had come very close to extinction in 1954 because of General Motors management's reservations about the car's sales potential. The attempt had been made, and the car had been built: Why not let the Corvette rest in the history books?

The reason: Thunderbird. Ford's two-seater arrived at the height of the perennial battle between the industry's two leading companies. For 18 months after mid-1953, Ford had engaged in production warfare, and it swamped its dealers with more cars than they could ordinarily sell. Ford was determined to become number one—even if it almost had to give away cars. GM naturally responded in kind, and the production blitz was on.

Both corporations took to the media. Each claimed victory, made counterclaims, and then accused the other of fudging the statistics. Nobody really knew who came out on top for 1955, but the competition was enough to change GM's attitude toward the Corvette. The two-seater field would not be left to the Thunderbird, which Corvette advertising soon referred to as a "scaled-down convertible."

Helping in its cause, GM had a 45-year-old German-trained enthusiast, race driver, designer, and engineer named Zora Arkus-Duntov on its staff. Since joining the GM Research and Development staff in 1953, Duntov had been fiddling with the Corvette in his

spare time. He had done some racing, and he knew what drivers of sporting cars demanded in their machines. Duntov described the early model's handling problems: "The front end oversteered; the rear understeered. I put two degrees of positive caster in the front suspension and relocated the rear spring bushing. Then it was fine; very neutral."

Those slight changes were typically Duntov. His seat-of-the-pants feel for what was right—and wrong—with the Corvette was to become legendary both inside and outside General Motors. In fact, his expertise became so respected that when it came to showdowns with management over his suggested changes, the white-haired wizard

Corvette's second generation showed some simplification in styling and stronger V-8.

usually won. "Fiddling" with the Corvette would become Duntov's life's work for the next 20 years. Moreover, the Corvette had found another ally just when it needed all the help it could get.

Duntov also described what happened when the Thunderbird appeared: "There were conversations...about the Corvette being dropped. Then the Thunderbird came out and all of a sudden GM was keeping the Corvette. I think that Ford brought out the competitive spirit in Ed Cole."

The 1956 Corvette was among the last GM production cars designed in Detroit before the design department was moved to the new Technical Center in Warren, Michigan. In a styling sense, the roots of the second-generation design were in three 1955 Motorama show cars—the Biscayne and two exercises dubbed LaSalle II. The Biscayne was a compact four-door hardtop painted light green with a color-keyed interior. Appearance features included headlamps mounted inboard, parking lights placed in the fenders, and a grille made up of a series of vertical bars. Air scoops were positioned under the windshield on the cowl, and the passenger compartment floor was level with the bottom of the frame. The LaSalle II name appeared on a hardtop sedan and a roadster. Also carefully color-keyed, both had prominent vertical bar grilles and

displayed a styling feature that the '56 Corvette would inherit—a concave section on the body sides. It swept back from the front wheel wells, imitating the "LeBaron sweep" of the classic period. The greenhouse used for the lift-off hardtop that would be a new option for 1956 was inspired mainly by a '54 show Corvette.

The '56 Corvette was all new, and it was beautifully done—not overdone, however. It curved in all the right places, with contours that looked smooth and purposeful. Many aficionados believe that it and the look-alike '57 were the most beautiful Corvettes of the pre-1963 period. Exterior colors offered were Onyx Black, Venetian Red, Cascade Green, Aztec Copper, Shoreline Beige, Silver, and Polo White.

Besides its attractive styling, the '56 offered several improvements in passenger comfort, probably in response to the sales drubbing Chevy's car had taken from the less sporty but more luxurious Thunderbird. Among them were roll-up door windows and the optional hardtop, which provided sedan-like weather protection and better visibility.

The 265-cid V-8 was again borrowed from the passenger car line, the six now permanently banished from the sports car. Like

the hottest standard Chevy mill, the Corvette's V-8 had a four-barrel carburetor and 9.25:1 compression ratio, but used a special high-lift cam developed by Duntov that raised horsepower to 225 at 5200 rpm and helped produce 270 foot-pounds of torque at 3600 rpm. The standard three-speed transmission and clutch were redesigned to handle the extra muscle. A 3.55:1 rear axle ratio was specified, but 3.27:1 gearing was optional. Powerglide automatic with the 3.55:1 cog was listed for $189 extra.

The performance of the '56 Corvette belied its civilized looks. With manual gearbox and standard axle ratio, the car would turn 0-60 mph in 7.5 seconds and run the standing-start quarter mile in 16 seconds at 90-plus mph. It was capable of close to 120 mph right off the showroom floor. Some questions still remained about handling and stopping, however.

The concave sides on the second-generation 'Vettes were taken from '55 Motorama show cars. Side windows now rolled up. (Above, owner: Pete Bogard)

Brakes—cast-iron drums with 158 square inches of lining area—were a weak point. They "faded into oblivion," as one tester said after a hard application. Handling was good, but understeer was ever-present. The steering, however, was quick—just 3½ turns lock-to-lock. Weight distribution, at 52/48, was nearly perfect for a sports machine. In all, road behavior was greatly improved.

1957

On the surface, the 1957 Corvette looked like the '56, but sported several significant under-the-skin changes—a larger V-8 option, a new four-speed gearbox introduced at mid-year, and (as Chevy boasted) up to one horse-power per cubic inch from the new "Ramjet" fuel injection system. Although developed by Rochester Carburetor, Ramjet was strictly a GM design. It incorporated a special aluminum manifold, a

fuel meter, and an air meter. The air meter directed the air to the various intake ports, where a precise amount of fuel was squirted in from a high-pressure pump driven off the distributor. Injection was available only for the new 283-cid enlargement of the 265, and gave it a rousing 283 bhp at 6200 rpm—the first time a mass-production engine developed one horsepower for each cubic inch of displacement. But the system had its bugs. Racing setups had to drop the fuel cutoff during acceleration to escape a flat spot; fuel nozzles absorbed heat and caused rough idling or suffered from dirt deposits. Street users found the system hard to service. Only 240 of the 6339 Corvettes built for 1957 were equipped with Ramjet. When feeling good, though, it provided staggering performance: 0-60 mph in about 6.5 seconds, for example.

The 283 was produced by boring the 265 block about ⅛-inch to 3.875 inches. It also had higher compression and a higher-lift cam.

Buyers had a choice of single (220 bhp) or dual (245 and 270 bhp) four-barrel carb setups plus two "fuelies" with 250 and 283 bhp. A racing version also had a nominal rating of 283 bhp. Valve lifters were hydraulic, except with injection. The 283 featured longer-reach spark plugs, carburetor fuel filters, larger ports, wider bearings, and oil-control piston rings. Dual exhausts on fuelies were con-nected by a crossover pipe, which equalized flow through each muffler, thus preventing uneven distribution and retarding rust.

A big step forward in Corvette performance was the May 1957 addition of a four-speed gearbox as a $188 option. It was essentially a three-speed Borg-Warner unit, with reverse moved into the tailshaft housing to make room for a fourth forward speed. The ratios were close at 2.20:1, 1.66:1, 1.31:1, and 1.00:1. Coupled to a fuelie engine and the optional 4.11 rear axle, it made the Corvette nothing less than a stormer. Tests showed 0-60

in 5.7 seconds, 0-100 in 16.8 seconds, the standing quarter mile in 14.3 seconds at 96 mph, and a top speed of 132 mph.

The experts still complained about handling and braking deficiencies, which Chevrolet solved with RPO 684, a comprehensive suspension package. It included front anti-sway bar and heavier springs; heavier rear leaf springs; larger, firmer shocks; ceramic-metallic brake linings with finned, ventilated drums; Positraction limited-slip differential; and a quick-steering adapter that reduced turns lock-to-lock from 3.7 to 2.9. Axle ratio options included 3.70:1, 4.11:1, and a root-pulling 4.56:1. With all of the options, you could order a car ready to race right out of the box—and race it did. Two production models finished 12th and 15th at Sebring 1957, the first GT-class cars across the line. The 12th place car ended up 20 laps ahead of the nearest Mercedes-Benz 300SL.

Undoubtedly, 1957 marked the Corvette's arrival as a sports car respected as much by the enthusiast as by the kids on the street. One European writer said: "Before Sebring, where we actually saw it for ourselves, the Corvette was regarded as a plastic toy. After Sebring, even the most biased were forced to admit that the Americans had one of the world's finest sports cars—as capable on the track as it was on the road. Those who drove and understood the Corvette could not help but reach that conclusion."

Now the survival of the Corvette could not be questioned. Model year production had risen from 3467 for 1956 to 6339 for '57. While the Corvette's place in the division lineup was now more or less assured, new approaches were in the works that would lead to a different kind of sports Chevy. For the car to continue, Chevrolet knew that it would have to make money, yet Corvette had not yet recorded a profit. Additional sales volume and customer appeal became the orders of the day.

In early 1957, General Motors had joined in the Automobile Manufacturers Association (AMA) resolution against any industry support for racing. All corporate competition efforts and publicity abruptly ceased. The policy, prompted by the National Safety Council and other groups, was based on the belief that racing activities and race-oriented automobile advertising inspired highway recklessness. The automakers officially withdrew from the sport for the next few years. And in one way or another, their change in attitude would eventually be reflected in their products.

Highlights of the 1956-57 restyling include two-toning, more chrome, side coves, smoother rear deck, frenched taillights.

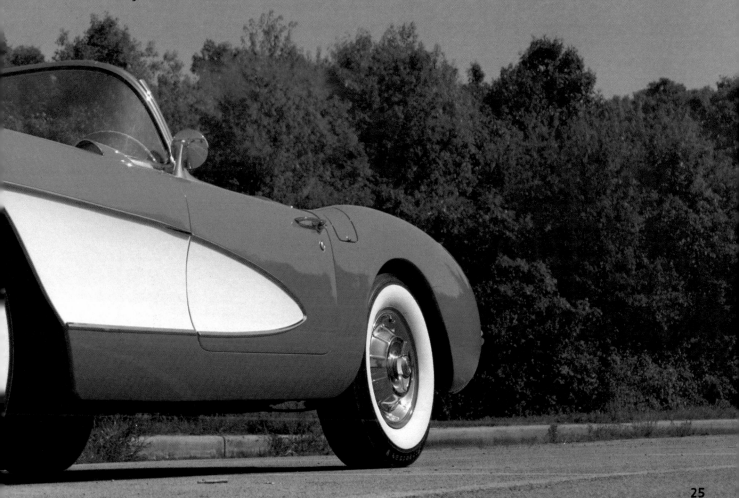

1958—62:
The Third-Generation Roadster

1958

The 1958 Corvette was typical of the new corporate stance. Styling was busier, and weight was up. It didn't look—and wasn't—as lithe and as agile as the 1956–57 models. Appearance changes were in keeping with then-current trends. The front sprouted four headlamps, with a chrome strip trailing back from each pair along the top of the fenders. Simulated louvers appeared on the hood, and chrome blossomed on the flanks, rear fenders, and trunklid. Overall length grew by nearly 10 inches, width by three inches. At 3000 pounds, the '58 weighed 100 pounds more than the '57.

Yet some useful changes had been made. At Duntov's behest, instruments were regrouped in a pod for better legibility. A large grab bar was added for the passenger, and seat belts were made standard. The fuel injection system was reworked for greater reliability, boosting output to 250 or 290 bhp at 6200 rpm. The carbureted 283s ranged from 230 to 270 bhp. The heavy-duty suspension option was retained.

1959

Styling stayed mostly the same for 1959. However, the fake hood louvers were erased, and Duntov saw to further detail refinements: Inside door knobs were moved forward to avoid snagging clothes, the shift lever received a lockout T-handle, and the clutch was given a wider range of adjustment. The RPO 684 suspension got even harder spring settings. Still working on the brake problem, Chevy issued RPO 686—sintered metallic linings—which cost only $27 and were well worth it. Radius rods were fitted to reduce rear axle tramp.

Despite its carryover design, the 1959 Corvette was a very desirable car. The cleaner body and strong powerplants combined to make a very nice package that could blow the doors off most any machine around. Many examples could shoot through the quarter-mile in less than 15 seconds, and 0-60 mph times of less than eight seconds were typical. By now, "fast car" and "Corvette" had become synonymous.

1960

The 1960 Corvette might have been a completely new car—the stillborn "Q" model, with all-independent suspension and a rear-mounted transaxle on a 94-inch wheelbase. The Q model's styling directly prefigured that of the 1963 Sting Ray. But difficult times precluded production, so the '60 was mostly a carryover of the '59.

However, more extensive use was made of aluminum—in clutch housings and some radiators, and in the cylinder heads of fuel-injected engines. The aluminum

heads were fine in theory, but suffered failures from internal flaws and tended to warp if the engine overheated. They were quickly dropped. Duntov replaced the stiff spring setup with double sway bars (the first rear suspension sway bar on an American car), which improved ride and handling. Only minor changes were made to the interior.

Corvette reached an international pinnacle at the 1960 Le Mans 24-hour race. Three cars entered by Briggs Cunningham in the big-engine GT class were excellent performers. One achieved 151 mph on the Mulsanne Straight, and the Bob Grossman/John Fitch car finished a respectable eighth. If Sebring '57 hadn't sufficiently impressed the Europeans, Le Mans '60 did.

1961

Styling for 1961–62 was a mild face-lift of the 1958–60, but highly effective. By that time, Bill Mitchell had relieved Harley Earl as chief of GM Design, and had created the racing Stingray, followed by the XP-700 show car. Both featured a new "ducktail" rear end; the show car's was combined with front and midsection roughly similar to that of the production 1958–60. The new tail received favorable reaction and appeared for '61. To help make the car still fresher, Mitchell did away with the teeth that had marked Corvette grilles since 1953, replacing them with a mesh screen. Headlamp rims were painted body color, also for a cleaner look.

Prices, meanwhile, had been climbing upward. The Corvette had listed (NADA base price) for $3149 in 1956, $3631 in 1958, and $3872 in 1960. For 1961, it was up to $3934. It would be $4038 in 1962. A fuel-injected car could run well over $5000—some $1500 above what you would have paid for a '53. For that kind of money, buyers expected a lot of standard equipment. Chevrolet obliged in

Opposite page, top: Third-generation 'Vettes were heavier, with quad lights. This one's fuel injected. Bottom: Rear chrome straps. Top: A '59 version. Above: The dash was arranged into two pods.

1961 by including an aluminum radiator, parking brake warning light, dual sun visors, interior lights, and windshield washers.

Engine options for '61 were a rerun of those from 1960. The four-speed manual gearbox received an aluminum case, and a wider choice of gear ratios was offered for the three-speed unit. More than 85 percent of Corvette buyers were now ordering manual transmissions, with a two-to-one preference for the four-speed when choosing manuals.

The hairy 315-bhp injected engine was truly impressive when coupled to stump-pulling rear axle ratios. With the 4.11:1 axle, a big-inch 'Vette could clock 0-60 mph in 5.5 seconds and run the quarter mile in 14.2 seconds at 99 mph. Despite the ultra-short gearing, the car could do almost 130 mph.

The 1958—61 period saw the last of the small-block Corvette V-8s, and no fewer than seven variations were offered during the period.

1961-62 rear styling (above) came from the '58 XP-700 (top).

28

Horsepower ratings ranged from 230 bhp to 315, having corresponding compression ratios from 9.5:1 to 11.0:1. Induction included one four-barrel carburetor, two four-barrel carburetors, and fuel injection for the different variations.

1962

For 1962, Bill Mitchell completed his styling refinements. He deemphasized the concave body side "cove" by eliminating its chrome outline and replaced the little teeth inside the reverse fender scoops with a grid. The mesh-type grille was blacked out, and a decorative strip of anodized aluminum was added to the rocker panels. The stiff springs were reinstated as an option; with their help, Dr. Dick Thompson won the SCCA A-production championship that year.

Semon E. "Bunkie" Knudsen replaced upward-bound Ed Cole as Chevrolet general manager, and he began to push for higher production. The result: 14,531 cars were built for 1962, as opposed to the 10,939 the preceding year. Corvette had turned the profit corner in 1958. Now it was making an adequate return on investment as well.

The car was also returning even better performance. The '62s featured a new 327-cid V-8 created by boring and stroking the 283 (4.00 × 3.25 inch), and the optional fuel injection was modified to suit. A 3.08:1 rear axle ratio was added for quiet cruising (available for the two lowest-horsepower engines only). The fine new powerplant formed the basis for Corvette muscle through 1965. For 1962 (and '63), it was available in four forms: 250 to 340 bhp with carburetion and 360 bhp with fuel injection. Improved torque gave the '62s better midrange performance, especially in the standing-start quarter mile. Typically, a 327 with the 3.70 differential would run it in 15 seconds at over 100 mph.

With the 1962 models, Corvette reached its peak of development. Thanks to Duntov, the car had long since shed whatever remained of its pedestrian origins. It was faster than ever, a superb handler, and functionally styled. With its new sintered-metallic brake linings, it could stop as well as it could go. It was also quite comfortable.

Corvette had received many important changes during its first 10 years, but none significantly altered the basic design. The X-braced frame and fiberglass body panels remained unaltered except in detail from 1953 through 1962. All of that changed with the 1963 Sting Ray. It was a revolution.

1963—67:
The Fourth-Generation Roadster

1963

In 1963, the Sting Ray was a revelation in its revolutionary form. In addition to the roadster body type, a beautiful new grand touring fastback coupe was introduced. Both roadster and coupe models sold more than 10,000 copies, putting total production for the model year at more than 21,500—about 50 percent better than any previous year. As the first of an entirely new line, the '63 has since received the recognition that it deserves as a landmark design.

Near the end of 1959, work had begun by GM Styling on the experimental project number XP-720, which would lead directly to the production 1963 Sting Ray. The XP-720 was based on Bill Mitchell's Stingray racer (*Stingray* spelled as one word, as it would be on production models after 1968). According to Duntov, the overriding goals for the project were "better driver and passenger accommodations, better luggage space, better ride, better handling, and high performance." As was usually the case with Duntov's projects, the "high performance" part of the project had highest priority.

The chassis for the XP-720 was entirely revamped, and the passenger compartment was placed as far back as possible. The center of gravity was lowered to promote improved handling and also enhance ride quality. Ground clearance ended up at just five inches, and the passengers now rode within the frame rather than on top of it. The center of gravity was 16.5 inches from the road, 2.5 inches less than on previous Corvettes. The 102-inch wheelbase also shrank, down to 98 inches. With major driveline components placed as low and close to the center as possible, the XP-720 emerged slightly tail-heavy, the rear

'63 'Vettes were influenced by Bill Mitchell's Stingray. (Owner: Santo Scafide)

wheels carrying 53 percent of the total static curb weight.

The old X-braced frame went by the boards in favor of a ladder-type design with five crossmembers. The design was chosen to ensure better torsional rigidity, an important consideration because of the minimum 300 bhp initially envisioned for the XP-720. The independent suspension that Duntov insisted on would increase lateral stress on the frame in hard cornering, thus requiring the extra torsional strength. At one point, though, frame stiffness was found to be more than the engineers needed. While it might help road-holding, it would exact a penalty in ride harshness. A compromise was

struck for production, providing more than adequate frame stiffness plus the desired ride characteristics. It was also less costly to build, no doubt an overriding concern, given the expense involved in switching to an independent rear suspension.

In fact, cost was the reason GM management used in attempting to talk Duntov out of independent rear suspension altogether. But Duntov would not compromise and, to justify its expense, he said that it would help Chevrolet move 30,000 Corvettes a year.

While Duntov was earnestly seeking an innovative and ultimately produceable new chassis, the stylists had only to clean up and refine the basic Stingray shape

that had been around for some three years. The earliest XP-720 mockups looked like nothing more than Mitchell's racer with a fastback roof. Wind tunnel testing helped to refine the shape, as did more practical matters like interior space, windshield curvatures, and tooling limitations. Both Mitchell's racer and the XP-720 were tested extensively in production-ready form at the Cal Tech wind tunnel.

Body engineers spent a great deal of effort on the inner structure of the XP-720. Compared with the '62 Corvette, the Sting Ray had nearly twice as much steel support built into its central body structure. But that additional weight was balanced by a reduction in fiber-

glass content, so the finished product actually weighed a bit less than a '62. Body features included curved door glass, cowl-top ventilation, increased luggage space, and an improved fresh-air heater. More than half of the roadsters were ordered with the optional lift-off hardtop, continued from previous years. Neither coupe nor roadster had an external trunklid as on the '62, which meant pulling the seatbacks down for access to the luggage space. The spare tire resided in an external hinged compartment that dropped down to ground level for access.

Other aspects of Mitchell's design were also interesting. Quad headlamps were retained, but now they were hidden, mounted in pivoting sections that fit flush with and matched the front-end contours. The Corvette was the first car with hidden lights since the 1942 DeSoto. Another DeSoto-type element (1955–56) was the "gull-wing" dash styling. "The dual cockpit was widely criticized at the time," one Corvette designer remembers, "but it was a very fresh approach to two-passenger styling."

Engines were carried over from 1962, but the brand-new body was matched by a modified chassis. Most of the changes were made at the back. For the first time, Corvette got independent rear suspension—a three-link type, with double-jointed open driveshafts on each side, plus control arms and trailing radius rods. A single transverse leaf spring (no room for coils) was mounted to the frame with rubber-cushioned struts, and the differential was bolted to the rear crossmember. The improved weight distribution resulted in better ride and handling, and axle tramp was virtually eliminated. A new recirculating-ball steering gear and three-link ball joint front

Opposite page: Bill Mitchell's Stingray racer has shark-like lines. Above: '63 production Sting Rays have similar lines.

33

suspension gave fewer turns lock-to-lock than before. Front brake drums were wider, and the brake system was now self-adjusting. Evolution dictated an alternator instead of a generator, positive crankcase ventilation, a smaller flywheel, and a new aluminum clutch housing.

Competition options for the Sting Ray were extensive, though designed mainly with the new coupe in mind, hinting that GM might be intent on becoming a GT-class and SCCA contender. The heavy-duty hardware included uprated springs and shocks, stiffer anti-sway bar, metallic brake linings, optional Al-Fin aluminum brake drums, cast aluminum knock-off wheels, dual master brake cylinder, and a 36.5-gallon fuel tank. Full leather upholstery became a new interior option—for the sales competition.

Road testers raved about the exotic-looking new Sting Ray, with special comments reserved for the improved traction. The new car neither hopped during hard acceleration nor oversteered on tight bends. It was quite impressive, with many of the niggling things that had been bothersome to buyers in the past having been reconciled.

In looking at Corvette history, the 1963 Sting Ray has a unique distinction: it was the only all-new model (apart from engines, which were only a year old anyway) between the original Motorama car of 1953 and the 1984 sixth-generation model. While the Sting Ray would undergo a very dramatic body revision just five years after it first hit the streets, the chassis would live on with only modest changes for a full two decades. That it did survive so long bespeaks the sophistication and foresight of its designers, especially Zora Arkus-Duntov.

1964

With Corvette sales increasing some 50 percent in a single year, logic dictated that changes for the follow-up 1964 edition would be only evolutionary in nature. The

two fake air intakes on the hood, which had been inspired by the genuine article on Mitchell's racer, were eliminated, although the indentations remained. The rocker panel trim lost some of its ribs, and the areas between the ribs were painted black. Wheel covers were simplified, and the fuel filler door gained concentric circles around its cross-flags insignia. In the cockpit, the color-keyed steering wheel was replaced with one with a simulated walnut rim. Complaints about glare from the instrument bezels were acknowledged, so they were painted flat black on the '64. Springs and shock absorbers were tweaked to provide a softer ride without sacrificing handling.

Again for '64, the Sting Ray was offered with a choice of four different versions of the 327-cid V-8, four different transmissions, and six axle ratios. The two least powerful engines were still rated at 250 and 300 bhp, both on 10.5:1 compression. The two high-performance mills received a few noteworthy improvements. The 340-bhp solid-lifter unit was massaged with a higher-lift, longer-duration camshaft to produce 365 bhp. The 360-bhp injected unit also gained another 15 horsepower, to 375. But this option cost a whopping $538, a sum that fewer

buyers were willing to spend. In the future, the route to 'Vette power would be through the time-honored expedient of more cubic inches, not injection. Positraction was still a bargain option in '64 at only $43.05, and more than 80 percent of production had it.

1965

Each of the Sting Ray years brought important mechanical advancements. For 1964, the fuel-injected 375-bhp small-block engine developed 1.15 bhp per cubic inch—enough for a 0-100 mph time of 15 seconds flat. For 1965, four-wheel disc brakes were offered optionally, something that enthusiasts had long been demanding, and made for awesome braking power. Also, '65 saw the introduction of another big boost to performance: the Mark IV V-8.

Big-engined Corvettes were nothing new, of course. Mickey Thompson's specials for Daytona and other races had been seen with the 409 engine as early as 1962. Zora Arkus-Duntov had at first resisted the idea of a big-block option, but by '64 the need was apparent. Cars like the Shelby Cobra were not outselling Corvette, but they were trouncing it in competition. Duntov teamed

with Jim Premo, who had replaced Harry Barr as Chevrolet chief engineer, to work the adaptation.

The first Mark IV displaced 396 cubic inches, mainly because GM policy in those days restricted cars of intermediate size and smaller to engines of less than 400 cid. Replacing the 365-bhp small-block option, it packed 425 bhp at 6400 rpm and 415 lbs/ft of torque at 4000 rpm, thanks to 11:1 compression, solid lifters, and a four-barrel carburetor. To handle the brute force, engineers added stiffer front springs, thicker front anti-sway bar, a new rear bar, heavier clutch, and a larger radiator and fan. Though the Mark IV engine weighed over 650 pounds, it did not adversely affect weight distribution, which remained near neutral at 51/49 percent front/rear. An aggressive-looking hood bulge and optional side-mounted exhaust pipes completed an impressive machine.

By the time Elliott M. "Pete" Estes had relieved Semon E. "Bunkie" Knudsen as Chevrolet general manager in 1965, the Corvette was permanently established in the divisional picture, with 20,000-plus sales a year. The production figures for each year of the Sting Ray indicate success.

The AMA's anti-performance resolution was ancient history in the mid-Sixties, and Chevrolet set about preparing a competition reply to the big-block Cobra. Its answer was the Grand Sport, with a special 377-cid aluminum block V-8. Only five cars were built, owing to GM's sudden cancellation of the project, which forced the Grand Sport to compete in SCCA class C-Modified. At Daytona 1963, all three Grand Sports ran 10 seconds a lap faster than the Cobras. Roger Penske won with one at Nassau the same year. Grand Sports were still racing as late as 1966, though by then they had been outclassed. The problem was not so much performance as numbers. Had Chevrolet been willing (and allowed by corporate higher-ups) to produce the minimum 100 cars necessary to qualify for a production class, the Grand Sport would have been unstoppable.

1966

For 1966, Duntov showed his L-88 option—a Mark IV bored to 427 cubic inches, developing 560 horsepower, the most powerful engine ever available for a Corvette. With a 4.11:1 gearset, it was capable of 0-60 mph in a nearly unbelievable 4.8 seconds,

0-100 in 11.2 seconds, and a maximum of 140 mph. The only car that could keep up with this Corvette was the 427 Cobra—and that was far less refined, with few of the Sting Ray's high-speed comfort features. Though the Cobra was a formidable competitor on the track, the big-inch Mark IV Corvette was really in a class by itself everywhere else.

The L-88 sat in a chassis featuring the now-famous F-41 suspension package, heavy-duty brakes, and Positraction. Unfortunately, the production Corvette just wasn't competitive in SCCA's A-production class. The Cobra had almost as much horsepower and was lighter by half a ton.

However, a place did exist for the big, strong, heavy Corvettes—endurance racing. In 1966, for example, Penske's team finished 12th overall and first in the GT class at the Daytona Continental. The next year, Dave Morgan and Don Yenko placed 10th overall

Opposite page: The '63 split-window coupe is one of the most collectible Corvettes. Above: A modified Sting Ray roadster prefigured future Sharks.

and first in GT at Sebring. Bob Bondurant and Dick Guildstrand actually led the highly competitive GT class at Le Mans for several hours until their engine blew sky high. Endurance racing held great promise for the big-block Corvettes, but their potential wasn't exploited.

By this time, Chevrolet was committed to providing underground support to Can-Am racers like Jim Hall and Trans-Am Camaro teams like Penske's. In effect, Chevy had abandoned the sports car classes to Shelby's Cobras, and went to play on a different field where it had a better chance of winning. Given the restrictions of the GM bureaucracy, it was impossible for Chevy to work with an outside contractor the way that Ford did with Carroll Shelby. It was equally impossible to turn a mass production car like the Corvette into an unqualified champion against hand-built machines created strictly for racing.

1967

Model year 1967 was supposed to see a brand-new Corvette. But the proposed styling turned out to have some undesirable aerody-

namic characteristics, and Duntov insisted that more time be spent in wind tunnel tests before it was approved for production. No brand-new Corvette seemed to make it into production on time.

Little more could be done than to soldier on with the Sting Ray, but the extra refinements made it perhaps the best of the breed. Styling was cleaned up—fake vents and extraneous emblems were gone. Five smaller front fender vents replaced the three on the '66, and less distracting flat-black and aluminum rocker panel moldings gave the car a lower, less chunky appearance. Unique to the '67 was a backup light above the license plate. Slotted six-inch-wide Rally wheels replaced the ornate wheel covers of earlier models, and were supplied with chrome beauty rings and lug nuts concealed behind small chrome caps. The cast-aluminum wheels were discontinued.

Inside, upholstery pleating was again changed slightly, and the handbrake lever was redesigned and moved from beneath the dash to the more convenient spot between the seats. For the first time, the convertible's optional hardtop was offered with a black vinyl covering.

The high-performance highlight for '67 continued to be the awesome L-88. Only 20 of the L-88s were produced, and not more than three are known to have survived. Other engine notes for the period of 1963–67 bear mentioning. Fuel injection was dropped after 1965, mainly due to high production costs, low sales, and the advent of the Mark IV program. Available engines for the five years were 327-cid, 396-cid, and 427-cid units which ranged from 250 to 435 brake horsepower.

The Sting Ray provided some of the most exciting motoring ever offered to Americans. The car was fast, very capable on any kind of road, and wonderful to look at. Unfortunately, it was the shortest-lived Corvette design of all. Yet it sold nearly 120,000 copies (72,418 roadsters) and remains among the most sought-after collector cars today. The Sting Ray brought Corvette development to a new peak of excellence and refinement.

This 1967 Corvette roadster has a big-block 427 Mark IV engine, rated at 400/435 brake horsepower for the model year. Note hood scoop and side pipes.

1968–75:
The Fifth-Generation Roadster

1968

The Sting Ray was hardly on the market a year when GM Styling Staff began planning its successor. It might actually have been a far different car from the one that emerged for 1968. Styling Staff had created a mid-engine design study, with a sharply raked front end, broad expanses of curved glass, skirted rear wheels, and nothing less than a functional periscope to serve as a rearview mirror. But over at Engineering Staff, the high cost of the necessary transaxle condemned the mid-engine configuration to the reject pile. Accordingly, the next series of production 'Vettes retained a very conventional mechanical layout, but bore a strong visual relationship to the experimental Mako Shark II show car of 1965.

The final styling work was directed by David Holls of the Chevrolet Studio, who couldn't have been a better choice. Holls had always been an automobile connoisseur and an enthusiastic driver as well as a talented stylist. His personality was reflected in the finished product. Holls kept the ground-hugging snoot of the Mako II, but notched its fastback roofline slightly and added a Kamm-style rear deck with a spoiler. One problem presented itself: air drag, which proved to be considerably greater than expected. Although the new design was scheduled to be introduced as a 1967 model, Duntov convinced division general manager Pete Estes to push it back to 1968 so that wind tunnel tests

The restyled fifth-generation 'Vettes (a 1968 model coupe shown on top) clearly reflected the design of the Mako Shark II show car (above).

37

could be made. The tests resulted in several changes: lower front fenders, a redesigned notchback, and a lower rear spoiler (the initial one had actually impeded air flow). Rear glass was also altered to improve visibility, and front fender louvers were enlarged to improve engine cooling and to reduce drag. An air dam was built into the front under-bumper pan, and pop-up headlights were hidden under panels that fit flush when closed.

The '68 Corvette retained the 1967 engine lineup, which meant that you could order Duntov's mighty L-88 racing powerplant with up to 560 horsepower. It featured aluminum heads with 12.5:1 compression, oversize valves, aluminum intake manifold, and a small-diameter flywheel with beefed-up clutch. The engine and its high-output descendants were not really street equipment, and very few were made.

At first, the '68 Corvette was not as well liked as it came to be—probably because the 1963–67 design was such a hard act to follow. The new body was seven inches longer (most of it in front overhang), though wheelbase remained at 98 inches. Yet the interior was more cramped than the Sting Ray's, and the '68 had less luggage space to boot. Some road testers bemoaned the new car's greater weight, up by 150

pounds compared with the '67. The car was criticized as being old-fashioned and overly gimmicky.

The sports car crowd still wasn't satisfied with the road engines. It attacked the car and V-8 engines as being unsophisticated and crude. Even so, a production record was set in 1968 with 28,566 units.

1969

Subsequent developments indicated that somebody was listening at General Motors. Duntov, who had been temporarily shunted aside from Corvette development, was restored to a position of considerable influence over the car's destiny. One change for 1969 was immediately evident: the Stingray designation (spelled as one word), which had disappeared

for 1968, again adorned the flanks. Exterior door handles were cleaned up, black-painted grille bars replaced chrome, and backup lights merged with the inner taillights. Handling was improved by wider-rim wheels, and a lot of shake was eliminated with a stiffer frame. The interior was reworked to create a bit more room for passengers and their odds and ends.

The small-block engine was stroked to 350 cid, and offered either 300 or 350 bhp (one horsepower per cubic inch was nothing new by 1969). Four 427-cid engines were fielded, together with a vast array of axle ratios, ranging from a super-low 4.56:1 to a long-striding 2.75:1. Duntov's racing version L-88 was joined by another mill—the aluminum-block ZL-1 dry-sump engine. It weighed 100 pounds less

than the L-88 and listed for an astounding $3000 in the option book. The L-88 and ZL-1 were the ultimate '69 Corvettes, but they were predictably few and far between. Division records show that only 116 L-88s and just two ZL-1s were completed during the year. On the other hand, thousands were delivered with the small-blocks, both very docile engines with more than enough pep.

1970

Chevrolet seemed to have its act together for 1970. Due to a strike, the '69 model run was extended two months longer than usual, which may have been the time that Chevy needed to make good with the '70. The strike was no doubt a factor in the '69 production record of almost 39,000 units (16,608 roadsters), but it also delayed the '70 from reaching dealer showrooms until February. That sent Corvette production plummeting to just 17,316 (6648 roadsters)—its lowest point since 1962.

Once again the major news was

under the hood. The LT-1 solid-lifter small-block appeared at last, boasting 370 bhp at 6000 rpm and a hefty $447.50 price. It differed from the lesser small-blocks in having more radical cam timing and valve lift, larger-diameter exhaust system, and the carburetor from the big-block engines, along with special cold-air hood intake. The lesser 350 V-8s returned, unchanged from their '69 specs. Reflecting the increasing stranglehold of emissions requirements, Chevy stroked the big-block to a full 4.00 inches for 454 cid. Output was 390 bhp at 4800 rpm on 10.25 compression. Also listed was the aluminum-head LS-7, a 465-bhp behemoth running 12.25:1 compression. Although ostensibly available to anyone, it was really a competition engine, and none were installed in regular production. It was capable of quarter-mile times in the 13-second range and terminal speeds near 110 mph.

Corvette cosmetics were again altered only in detail for 1970. The extreme bodyside tuck-under on the 1968–69 models was found to

be susceptible to stone damage, so Chevy flared the aft portions of each wheel opening, which helped to some degree. The grille—actually false, as the radiator air intake was on the car's underside—was changed from horizontal bars to an egg-crate pattern, and the parking lamps changed from small round units to clear-lens, amber-bulb rectangular fixtures. The grille pattern was repeated on the front fender vents, replacing the four "gills" used before. The dual exhaust outlets also shifted from round to rectangular.

Inside, the seats were reshaped to provide better lateral support, more headroom, and easier access to the still-lidless cargo bay. The

Opposite page, top: The XP-882 experimental car had a mid-engine layout. Bottom: From '70 to '72, Stingray styling featured eggcrate side vents and grille. Above: T-top coupe sales cut into roadster sales.

shoulder belts, separate from the lap belts, got inertia storage reels, ending some cockpit clutter. A deluxe interior group was added to the options list, consisting of full cut-pile carpeting and ersatz wood trim on the console and doors.

The days of big-inch, big-power Corvettes were already numbered. During the Seventies, both horsepower and displacement would fall. As they did, America's sports car would become a more balanced package that would satisfy enthusiasts.

1971

The future arrived with a thud for 1971, when GM ordered an across-the-board compression drop so that all of its engines could run on low- or no-lead fuel. The 'Vette didn't escape, and the results were dramatic. Compression in the small-block V-8 now ran a mild 8.5:1, packing only 270 bhp at 4800 rpm. Compression on the LT-1 sighed to 9.0:1, with rated output sinking to 330 bhp at 5600 rpm. The same compression numbers were applied to the big-blocks, with the LS-5 rated 365 bhp at 4800 rpm and the LS-6 rated 425 bhp at 5600 rpm.

None of the engines was exactly a weakling. Relative to the prodigious power of the engines developed for the muscle car era, the Corvettes weren't as strong, but they remained exceptionally fast next to most other cars on the road. Predictably, the open-chamber-head LS-6 was the top dog, capable of pushing from 0-60 mph in less than 5.5 seconds, with the quarter-mile shooting by in just under 14 seconds at 105 mph. Top speed was claimed to be in excess of 150 mph. The somewhat milder LS-5 was good for quarters in the low 14s with automatic, and was only marginally slower in the 0-60 mph test.

Virtually no styling changes were made on the '71s. But some significant engineering was applied. The ZR-1 package was offered—a racing package. It consisted of the LT-1 small-block, heavy-duty four-speed transmission and power brakes, aluminum radiator, and a revised suspension with special spring, shocks, stabilizer bar, and spindle strut shafts. It could not be ordered with power windows,

The 1975 model year was the last one in which the roadster was offered until the '86 model year. The soft nose ('73–'75) and tail ('74–'75) became part of the styling.

power steering, air conditioning, rear window defroster, wheel covers, or radio. Only eight of them were built.

With sales recovering, the coupe was selling at a 5:3 ratio to the roadster. Coupes had taken the sales lead from the roadster beginning in 1969, perhaps reflecting the T-top model's greater all-weather versatility. Convertible popularity was on the wane throughout the industry, and the government seemed ready to enact a safety standard for rollover protection in a crash which would have effectively made the sale of fully open cars illegal in the United States after 1975. All of these factors conspired against the romantic 'Vette roadster, which had only a couple of years left to run.

1972

Corvette mainly marked time for 1972. Engines now bore the full brunt of emissions tuning, with the result that both horsepower and performance were deemphasized even further. The big-block LS-6 option was cancelled, leaving the 365-bhp LS-5 the most potent engine in the lineup.

The fiber-optic light monitors were deleted from the center console, cleaning up the console considerably. The anti-theft alarm system previously offered at extra cost was made standard, in recognition of the high appeal of the 'Vette to thieves.

1973

The first major styling change in the fifth generation arrived for 1973—a new "soft" body-colored nose designed to meet the

government's five-mile-per-hour front-impact protection rule. The new system—a steel bumper covered by deformable urethane plastic—added only 2.2 inches to the Corvette's overall length and 35 pounds to the curb weight. Altogether, it didn't look too bad. Another piece of mandated safety equipment was steel reinforcement beams in the doors to protect against side impact.

In addition, radial tires were now standard equipment, but they delivered poorer performance than the bias-belted ones. Rated at a lower speed level than previous ones had been, the tires were a disappointment. The engine options were two, and both were bogged down by smog and safety hardware.

1974

The 'Vette appeared again mostly

unchanged for 1974. A lot of people began to wonder if the design had been frozen. It had not, of course, but the marketing approach had changed along with the car's character. Corvettes were now much more expensive, appealing to a different clientele. The 350-cid open model with 250 net bhp started at $5500, and usually sold for $800 to $1000 more than that. It also weighed about 3500 pounds. It was a far cry from the light and nimble Sting Rays. Instead of hairy-chested performance, it was oriented more to comfortable touring. But production was up, and would continue rising in the years ahead.

The '74s did have some un-obtrusive changes, mainly to meet federal regulations. The original Kamm-like tail was replaced with an energy-absorbent rounded shape that was less effective at holding down the rear end. The consensus was that the loss in rear end adhesion didn't matter much, given the decline in out-right performance. One bright spot was the "gymkhana" suspension using the tried-and-true formula of

employing high-rate springs and firmer shocks. Luxury options proliferated: electric windows, vacuum-assisted brakes, integrated air conditioning, stereo tape deck, and leather upholstery. Even with all of the options, a 350-cid Corvette could still do 0-60 mph in 7.5 seconds and easily exceed 125 mph. It also returned about 14 mpg—by Corvette standards, an improvement in economy.

1975

Model year 1975 saw no obvious physical changes in America's sports car. The big-block V-8, which had first been wedged into a Corvette for 1965, was dropped altogether, a casualty of the oil wars. The only optional engine was now the L-82 small-block, rated at 205 bhp (SAE net), and the base 350 was detuned to a measly 165 bhp. To keep the power ratings from being even more anemic, the switch was made to catalytic converters, a move made by most automakers in '75. A positive note was the advent of breakerless electronic ignition,

accompanied by an electronic tachometer drive. Outside, small extrusions with black pads were added to the front and rear bumpers. A headlamps-on warning buzzer was added per Washington dictates. Sales hit 38,465.

A milestone of sorts was hit in '75: It would be the last year for the genuine Corvette roadster. Since the 1953 original, the roadster style had been a big part of the Corvette tradition, but GM was up against declining interest in convertibles generally and a rising chorus of safety-firsters. The last of 4629 ragtops came off the line in July, the end of an era. . .at least for a while.

The roadster would return. However, radical changes would be made and ten years would pass before the top would fold down on the body of another production Corvette.

Only 4629 roadsters were built for model year 1975. Heading into the sunset, they were overweight and underpowered.

1984:
The Sixth-Generation Corvette

A great deal of development went into the most recent Corvette generation—both engineering and styling. In order to have an understanding of the 1986 roadster, an all-around look at the coupe on which it is based and that coupe's history is in order.

Like the fabled Sting Ray of a generation ago, virtually every part of the latest 'Vette was all new except for the engine and one transmission, and even there some revisions were made. According to Chevrolet Division general manager Robert C. Stempel, the 1984 Corvette represented the closest collaboration between Engineering and Styling yet seen on a GM car. The chief collaborators were David R. McLellan, director for all Corvette engineering since Zora Arkus-Duntov retired in 1975,

and Jerry R. Palmer, the head of Chevrolet Studio Three and one of the stylists responsible for the sleek Aerovette show car of the early Seventies which served as the takeoff point for the '84's styling.

Above: An early prototype shows that minor changes were made—the rear end treatment, for instance. Below: Sixth and first generation 'Vettes lead examples of fourth and fifth.

Engineering

According to McLellan, the engineering keynote was "form follows function." McLellan and his team deemed following that dictum absolutely essential for the new Corvette to be competitive with other, more recently designed sports cars like the Porsche 928 and the Datsun 280-ZX. Specifically, the task was to eliminate the deficiencies for which the fifth-generation 'Vette had been criticized while at the same time maintaining the traditional Corvette look and feel. And the new car had to have superior aerodynamics, more passenger room, and—most important for a driver's car—better handling response compared to earlier models.

The sixth-generation Corvette was engineered literally from the ground up—around a pivot point. The so-called "T-point" defines the position of the seated driver's hip joint in relation to the interior and the rest of the car. For the new model, the T-point was raised about an inch and moved an inch or so rearward compared with the previous Corvette, on the assumption that the most important person is the driver. The change opened up more legroom and also put the driver higher in relation to the road surface for better visibility. Further, it enabled the chassis to sit higher than before for greater ground clearance, though the use of 16-inch rather than 15-inch wheels also played a part.

The ground-up engineering extended to the wheels and tires. As McLellan put it: "The handling of the car is dominated by its tires as well as its structural integrity." The 1984 Corvette rode on a new radial developed specifically for it by Goodyear—the Eagle VR50, in a massive P255/50VR-16 size. The "VR" part of the designation refers to one of several speed ratings for tires used in Europe, specifically those designed for speeds in excess of 140 mph, which the '84 'Vette could attain. Mounted on aluminum wheels of 8.5-inch width front and 9.5-inch width rear, the tires featured what Goodyear called a "gatorback" tread design intended to shed water more effectively to resist hydroplaning in wet weather. The Eagle VR50s were also intended to be unidirectional, owing to the shape of the wheels' radical cooling fins—the left and right wheels were not interchangeable, and neither were the front and rear. The gatorbacks gave the new Corvette phenomenal cornering capability. Equipped with the optional Z51 Performance Handling Package, the '84 Corvette was capable of up to .95g lateral acceleration on the skidpad.

The revised chassis had as much to do with the demon cornering ability as the tires. Chevy abandoned its traditional perimeter-type frame for a new steel "backbone" design not unlike that used by Colin Chapman in his various Lotus cars. In the Corvette, however, the "spine" took the form of a C-section beam that carried the propshaft and was connected rigidly to the differential. The benefit of the configuration was less weight and more cockpit room, through the elimination of

Opposite page: The aerodynamic sixth-generation Corvettes were first introduced as targa-topped coupes. Left: The Corvette badge has undergone as many changes as the car.

transmission and differential crossmembers. It also allowed the exhaust system to run under the propshaft instead of alongside it.

Welded to the frame was an "integral perimeter-birdcage unitized structure"—"uniframe," for short—making the new model the first to employ unitized construction instead of separate body-on-frame. The "birdcage" formed the windshield and door frames, lower A-pillar extensions, rocker panels, rear cockpit wall, and front subframe. It also included the "hoop" at the rear of the cockpit, which acted as the attachment point for the back window of the coupe. The entire structure was galvanized inside and out for corrosion resistance and acted as a skeleton for hanging major body panels, which were still made of fiberglass. Completing the basic assembly was an aluminum bolt-on front bumper carrier. A similar bolt-on extension supported the back bumper.

To match the new chassis, Chevy gave the '84 Corvette a heavily reworked suspension. The front end retained the familiar unequal-length upper and lower A-arm arrangement of previous years, but with a new twist. Instead of a coil spring on each side, the '84 had a single fiberglass-reinforced plastic leaf

spring mounted transversely between the two lower arms. A 20mm anti-roll bar was standard; a 25mm bar was a part of an optional handling package. At the rear was a newly designed five-link setup, with upper and lower longitudinal links mounted between the hub carriers and the body, twin lateral strut rods connecting the differential with the hub carriers, another transverse plastic leaf spring, plus U-jointed halfshafts and rear-mounted tie rods.

New to the Corvette for '84 was rack-and-pinion steering, replacing the previous recirculating-ball type. The new steering featured a

forward-mounted rack for greater precision and high-effort power assist for better control at higher speeds. The standard steering ratio was a constant 15.5:1, quite fast for an American car. With the optional Z51 handling package, that went up to 13:1. A tilt-and-telescope steering wheel was standard equipment.

As before, stopping power came from big vented disc brakes at each wheel, hydraulically assisted as standard. However, the brakes themselves were a new design created by Girlock, an American offshoot of the British Girling company. Making extensive use of

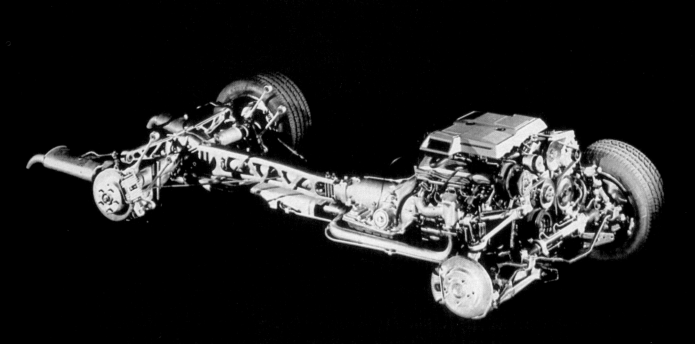

Opposite page, top left and right: Suspension pieces of the sixth-generation 'Vette are made of aluminum. Bottom: The chassis of the 1984 model year Corvette is based on a central backbone, a departure from the perimeter and ladder frames employed by earlier models. Left: The dashboard has electronic analog and digital speedometer and tachometer to either side of the steering column, with other information in the center. Bottom: The sixth-generation design underwent wind tunnel testing.

aluminum, the brakes had 11.5-inch rotors and featured quick-change semimetallic pads and audible wear sensors.

Dave McLellan took a personal interest in the new Corvette's chassis development: "Even in base suspension configuration, the new Corvette . . . is absolutely superior to any production vehicle in its part of the market." To ensure that the '84 Corvette lived up to his claim, McLellan and company developed a handling option for the new car—the Z51 Performance Handling Package. It consisted of the Eagle VR50 tires (a mandatory option with the base suspension),

heavy-duty shocks front and rear (RPO F51), and the FE7 Sport Suspension with heavy-duty lower control arm bushings, uprated front and rear springs and stabilizer bars, plus the faster-ratio steering. A shorter 3.31:1 rear axle was also included.

Under the '84 Corvette's long, shapely "clamshell" hood was a familiar friend in somewhat different dress—the trusty Chevy 5.7-liter/350-cid V-8 in its L-82 form, with twin throttle-body electronic fuel injection, the so-called "Cross-Fire" induction system with dual ram air intakes introduced on the 1982 model. In

appearance, the underhood area was dominated by a flat-top, silver-finish air cleaner cover made of die-cast magnesium. Though its ductwork has since been replaced, its silver and black coloring heightened the high-tech appearance of the engine compartment.

For the first time in several seasons Corvette's standard transmission was a four-speed manual unit. But it wasn't anything like previous manuals. It was a normal gearbox with a second planetary gearset attached, actuated by the engine's Computer Command Control electronics. The auxiliary gearset sat at the rear of

the transmission and engaged in all ratios except first through a hydraulic clutch. The effect was to provide "overdrive" reduction of .67:1 in each of the top three cogs to keep engine speed down, thereby benefiting part-throttle fuel economy. At wide throttle openings the overdrive gearing was automatically locked out. The standard final drive or rear axle ratio was 2.73:1, with 3.07:1 or 3.31:1 gearing available for more off-the-line punch. Chevy found that it needed the taller "overdrive" gearing in the intermediate ratios for the new 'Vette to achieve figures sufficiently high to avoid coming under the dreaded "gas guzzler" tax.

Returning from '82, but now as an option, was a four-speed overdrive automatic transmission. It was the GM 700-R4 unit with lockup torque converter clutch, familiar in the firm's full-size cars for the previous few years but new to Corvette for '82.

Despite Chevy's considerable effort to reduce the Corvette's weight, the '84 model was still fairly hefty. True, it weighed some 250 pounds less than a comparably equipped '82, itself no lightweight, but the '84 model's quoted base curb weight of 3117 pounds was still a good 300 pounds more than many observers had predicted and hoped for. Chevrolet engineers managed to keep weight down through new applications of lightweight materials. Some of them were industry firsts: The propshaft and yokes, for instance, were made from forged aluminum, welded together. Another first was a radiator support made of sheet molding compound (SMC) that incorporated a 27-percent "bubble" filler. The fiberglass-strengthened plastic springs front and rear purported to weigh half as much as four coil springs of comparable size, and were also claimed to be more durable—able to withstand 5,000,000 full cycles without failure, compared with about 75,000 cycles for conventional steel springs. The new cooling system had twin expansion tanks made of plastic, as were the radiator fan and shroud. Aluminum figured extensively elsewhere—the front suspension control arms and knuckles, the rear suspension's lateral control arms, the chassis's central "spine" beam, the torque converter housing, the brakes' splash shields, and the brake calipers.

Fascinating technical details? No doubt—enough to captivate enthusiasts every bit as much as previous 'Vettes, if not more.

Styling

For more than a decade, many Corvette fans have said that General Motors made a mistake by not putting the sleek, mid-engine Aerovette show car into production. But the press kit had this to say about the 1984 Corvette: "The totally new Corvette began to take shape in [Jerry R.] Palmer's studio in 1978, but it has its roots in a Chevrolet show car that took

shape as long ago as 1972." That reference was to Aerovette, the design that inspired the sixth-generation production car.

Jerry Palmer has been chief stylist at Chevrolet's Studio Three since 1974. It was about a year before he assumed that post that the Aerovette was shown publicly in its original form. Palmer remembered the car: "In the early Seventies, we were thinking along the line of a mid-engine sports car as our next Corvette. Work on

Below: The open targa top of the newest generation of Corvettes provides fresh air. The top is opened across the entire cockpit, leaving the hatch window in place. Above: A coupe open for inspection.

such a car accelerated when the rotary engine was viewed as a promising powerplant for a sport machine. We designed a car which was dubbed '4-Rotor' after its powerplant and, since this was a concept car, we experimented with a lot of new things—gullwing doors, a windshield angled in plan view, and a more practically aerodynamic shape than anything we'd designed before."

The "4-Rotor" was one of several GM experimentals seen in the late Sixties and early Seventies that were designed to test both the feasibility of the mid-engine configuration and, later, a new GM-designed engine based on Felix Wankel's principles. Zora Arkus-Duntov did the chassis and trans-axle engineering for the initial prototype, XP-882, built around Oldsmobile Toronado mechanicals, and the mere fact that he was involved in such a project led many observers to conclude that a mid-engine 'Vette was just around the corner.

Then the Arab Oil embargo hit late in 1973, and the first "energy crisis" was on. The crisis only highlighted the Wankel engine's unusual thirst for fuel relative to displacement. GM quickly shelved plans for both its rotary engine and the cars designed around it.

But the four-rotor exercise still had some life in it. A few years later it was taken off the shelf, fitted with a standard Chevrolet V-8, and retitled *Aerovette*. That name started rumors flying once more, and Bill Mitchell did his best to be sure that they came true. He lobbied hard with Chevrolet management, and actually won approval from then-chairman Thomas Murphy to put the design into production as the 1980 Corvette.

Then came a change of heart. For one thing, the car's most ardent supporters—Mitchell, former Chevrolet chief and GM president Ed Cole, even Zora Duntov—had all left the company by 1977. Also, Chevy was still able to sell every old-style Corvette that the St. Louis plant could build, so division managers quite logically saw little need

for a replacement, let alone such a radical one.

But the Aerovette wasn't dead yet. A new Corvette program was started in early 1978, shortly after the Aerovette-based model was cancelled. The designers kept coming back to that stunning shape. Although certain of its elements—gullwing doors, mid-engine package, vee'd wind-shield—were immediately ruled out on cost and production feasibility grounds, the Aerovette's basic styling "philosophy" became the starting point for what would become the 1984 production car.

Soon a basic package was laid down, and the designers were given some very hard instructions.

First and foremost was the demand that the new car must look like a Corvette. In other words, it couldn't break with traditional 'Vette appearance "cues" as radically as Aerovette had. Because drivelines would be basically carryover items, the new car would also have to continue the tradi-tional front-engine/rear-drive layout. So the midships 'Vette disappeared. The new car could be a bit smaller outside, but it had to have more room inside. It also must have a hatchback. Other parts of the design brief were that the car have improved forward visibility, more luggage space, and an obviously driver-oriented dashboard and control layout. Finally, the new

'Vette should have reduced aerodynamic drag.

What emerged after some four years was a car that was recognizably new, but still very much a Corvette. Palmer described it: "I really believe we've designed a car without compromises, but we've managed to retain the Corvette identity. The new car still, for example, has folding headlamps. It has a Corvette 'face,' even though there are fog lamps and park and turn lamps where air intakes used to be. The front fender vents are still there as is the large backlight and the functional rear spoiler. The first time people see this car, they're going to know what it is. They're going to say, 'Hey,! That's a new

Corvette!'" Palmer also thought that "people are going to be amazed when they see this car for the first time. But they'll be even more amazed when they see it next to an '82 Corvette. The new car's massive surfaces, such as the hood, are deceiving. On first glance, you probably wouldn't believe it is smaller than the previous year's model in every dimension except width."

Palmer was both right and wrong. While some of the dimensional reductions in the '84 line weren't that great, others were, and they were the ones to make the new car's proportions fresh yet familiar. Overall length, for example, was down a significant 8.8 inches

from the '82, despite only a two-inch cut in wheelbase (from 98 to 96 inches) and a mere 1.7-inch reduction in front overhang. The secret was rear overhang, which had been chopped a noticeable 5.2 inches, giving the new Corvette the illusion of having a longer hood, even though it was actually shorter. Contributing to the

Opposite page, top: The experimental 4-Rotor Corvette was named after its proposed four-chamber rotary engine. Bottom: The '84's 350-cid engine. Above: The new 'Vettes are front engine, rear drive.

51

sleekness was a very "fast" 64-degree windshield angle, the sharpest on any U.S. GM car, though, interestingly, it wasn't as laid back as the 60-degree slope on the 1983 Ford Thunderbird. Compared with the '82 Corvette, the base of the windshield now sat 1.5 inches lower and a little further forward which, in turn, allowed the beltline to be dropped, thus giving the '84 a glassier appearance.

But Palmer suggested that the real change in the sixth-generation 'Vette's appearance came from the increase in width. The old pinched-waist midsection had been allowed two inches of middle-age spread, giving the body a smoother, more massive contour, especially when viewed from the front or rear three-quarter angle.

Another marked difference in the 1984 styling concerned the Corvette's trademark arched fenders. The new car retained its predecessor's flared wheel opening lips, which together with the fat tires accentuated the hunkered-down look. But the front fender bulges were considerably toned down, and they blended smoothly into the beltline rather than con-flicting with it. The line rose gently from the base of the wind-shield toward the near-vertical Kamm-type tail over the rear wheel openings, where there was virtually no bulge at all. The result, in profile, was a slight but discernible wedge shape that was organic and functional in the GM idiom.

One styling element new to Corvette was a perimeter rub strip that completely encircled the car and served visually to link the tops of the front and rear bumpers. It also helped to conceal the shut lines for the new "clamshell" hood, which wrapped down along the body sides to about the top third

of the front wheel openings.

The new 'Vette was a "bottom breather," meaning that its engine intake air entered from beneath the car—in this case from a point below the front bumper just ahead of a modest lip spoiler. Although underhood ducting of that air has changed, the early ducting is still echoed externally as "power bulges."

Chevy boasts that the final shape of the 1984 Corvette was at least partly determined in the wind tunnel. One new wrinkle in the car's development was the use of sensors to measure pressure in the wind tunnel. The measurements noted differences between the pressure at various points on the car as it lay in a moving airstream and the pressure on other places in the tunnel. The result, says Chevy, was a detailed picture of the "actual pressure variants and vortices created by passage of the vehicle. Such an image is far more useful to designers than is a picture of surface flow only, and Corvette is believed to be the first sports car ever designed with the assistance of such a tool."

With all of that, the newest-generation Corvette might have been expected to have an impressively low coefficient of drag (Cd), but in fact it didn't. The claimed value for the coupe was "only" 0.34, good by contemporary standards, but not great. Though the figure does represent a 23.7 percent drag reduction compared with the 1982 Corvette's 0.44 Cd, it still trailed Chevy's own new-generation Camaro Z-28s and Pontiac Firebird Trans Am by a couple hundredths of a point—surely a bit of a letdown for owners of the new 'Vette.

On the other hand, those owners probably found that the newest 'Vette was the easiest ever to live with, and the most practical. Despite the shorter wheelbase and a reduction in overall height, the sixth-generation 'Vette offered fractional gains in head and leg room, along with a whopping 6.5-inch increase in total shoulder room—a dimension where the old Corvette was decidedly tight.

The cockpit also underwent a total redesign. It was dominated by a very space-age instrument panel and the usual tall center tunnel/console. Occupants actually sat a bit lower in the new 'Vettes. All instrumentation was directly ahead of the driver—no more minor dials in the center of the dashboard. In fact, no dials could be found at all: the new Corvette used an all-electronic display supplied by GM's AC Division. Digital and analog displays showed road speed and engine speed, while minor functions were monitored as numerical readouts in a smaller panel flanked by the two main displays. A switch panel in the vertical portion of the center console allowed the driver to select which functions would be monitored. Functions included such things as instantaneous and average miles per gallon, trip odometer, and fuel range, all of which were calculated by the on-board engine computer. The console also housed the sound system controls, a warning light panel, and heating/ventilation controls.

The standard seats in the new Corvette were newly designed high-back buckets with prominent bolsters on both cushion and backrest, manual fore/aft adjustment and backrest recline, and full cloth trim. Leather upholstery was offered at extra cost. Also optional was the latest in "super seats," supplied by the Lear/Siegler company. They provided electric adjustment for backrest angle and cushion bolster in/out position, plus a power three-stage lumbar support adjuster using inflatable "bladders" that could be selectively air-bled to achieve the proper contour.

Jerry Palmer summed up the design story: "When we set out to create the new Corvette, we set aside flashiness and concentrated on basics, like cleanliness, comfort, and function. I think this new Corvette is a statement of that principle. It will be a joy to drive and own, and it will appear stylish on the road five or ten years from now."

Opposite page: The '84 model 'Vettes owed their design to several experimental and show cars. Left: An '84 Corvette's interior, with automatic transmission gear selector.

Corvette Roadster People

Over the years, the Corvette roadster has owed its style, design, engineering—its very existence—to a special group of people who have worked for General Motors. The 33 years of the car's life rightfully may be credited to many, but a few of the people stand out in its history.

Harley Earl: The Father

Harley Earl is generally conceded to be the person who gave impetus to the first Corvette. The fiberglass-bodied two-seater probably could not have progressed from Motorama dream car to production reality without Earl's backing. He fought for the Corvette from the very first, against some fairly stiff odds, and for a reason: it was his sort of car.

While working as a designer of horse-drawn coaches in Los Angeles, Harley Earl had been hired as a consultant to GM by the general manager of Cadillac, Lawrence P. Fisher, when Earl was 32 years old. One of Earl's first assignments was body design for the 1927 LaSalle, the first edition of Cadillac's "companion" make. It became the first mass-produced car to be "styled" in the modern sense.

That first LaSalle proved an instant hit, and Earl was soon invited by president Alfred P. Sloan, Jr., to work for the company full time, with the specific task of setting up an in-house styling department—duly organized as the Art & Colour Section (the English spelling for *color* being Earl's way of connoting prestige). The department was an industry first.

Sloan and Fisher had been impressed by Earl's total approach to his work. For example, he pioneered the use of modeling clay to evolve the forms of various body components, and in those days clay was considered a highly unusual material for the purpose. Earl also created complete automobiles, with the main body, hood, fenders, lights, and other parts conceived in relation to each other so as to blend into a harmonious whole. The method contrasted with that of most custom bodybuilders, who usually worked from the cowl back, leaving a car's "stock" hood, radiator, and headlamps pretty much intact.

The impact of Earl and his assembled staff of bright designers on the shape of GM cars was enormous. In fact, it may be said that for most of his 31 years with the company, the GM design philosophy and Earl's philosophy were one and the same. He was an exuberant and unexpectedly playful person.

His elfishness contrasted sharply with Earl's physical stature. He was

a large man, standing over six feet tall. Because his height gave him a visual perspective that most of his designers lacked, they would often do their modeling while standing on wooden boxes to view their efforts the way that he would see them—though never in his presence.

"That's all I want [my designers] to do—start exercising their imaginations," he once said. "The ideas will soon pop up." Earl's own imagination was formidable, yet it was always tempered by a shrewd understanding of popular taste honed by contact with the public at the GM Motoramas and other events.

Earl liked nothing better than working on flashy show cars. He personally designed many of the Motorama experimentals that can still be remembered so well today, including the original Corvette.

In essence, Harley Earl liked to do things his way, and he usually had the wherewithal to accomplish them. He never lost his enthusiasm for cars during his long career with GM, right up to his retirement in 1958. Of course, the long, hard fight for the Corvette came toward the end of that career, a fight that would continue through the Corvette's difficult infancy.

William L. Mitchell: Mr. Sting Ray

Few automotive designers have been as powerful or as influential as William L. Mitchell. Certainly none have been more outspoken. In 1958, Mitchell became head of what was then called the General Motors Styling Staff, taking over for another larger-than-life figure—his mentor Harley Earl. Over the next 20 years, he would be responsible for the design of more than half the cars and trucks sold in the United States, not to mention a host of other GM products ranging from refrigerators to diesel locomotives.

Of course, no one could hope to attain such enormous responsibility without talent. And even his detractors readily admitted that Mitchell was blessed with that in abundance. Controversial, highly visible, and never given to halfway measures, Mitchell pulled few punches in his work, his arguments over policy with GM managers, or his public pronouncements—especially concerning automotive design.

Bill Mitchell ended up designing automobiles almost by accident. As a youth he was no doubt at least partly inspired by his father, who operated a Buick dealership in Pennsylvania. During the early Thirties, young Mitchell secured a job as an illustrator for the Barron Collier advertising agency in New York City. He spent some of his spare time drawing cars.

After he got to know Mr. Collier and his three sons, Mitchell began spending time with them at the race track they owned at Sleepy Hollow in upstate New York. At one of the races, he met someone who saw his sketches and asked if Mitchell would be interested in designing cars. "He said, 'I know a big fellow named Harley Earl who's the head of styling at General Motors.'" Before long, Mitchell sent some of his sketches to Detroit, and received a letter from Earl asking what the young illustrator thought cars "ought to look like in the future." Mitchell received the letter in the summer of 1935, and, he recalls, "in December of 1935 I was

at work at General Motors."

Some have even gone so far as to credit him with raising industrial design from profession to fine art, and there is ample evidence to support that view. His very first production automotive design, for example, was the 1938 Cadillac 60 Special sedan, recognized today as one of the most significant styling achievements of the late prewar era. Later, Mitchell was the creative force behind such memorable production cars as the 1963 Buick Riviera and stunning show models like the Corvair Monza GT and SS. But perhaps his greatest achievement—certainly his greatest love—was the Corvette, specifically the Sting Ray of 1963.

About the Sting Ray: "I just took all those lines and turned the Stingray, which is what I called the racer, into [the production 1963 Sting Ray]. That made the Corvette. And overnight the sales just boomed. So I knew I had something. I fought like hell to get that strut down the back [window]. Duntov didn't want it.

"I had to admit [the strut] was a hazard. Duntov won that one. By the way, I stole that back line from the Porsche. I wasn't above stealing things from European cars. Not American cars—nothing over here to steal. . . You need identity on a car.

"I love sharks because, in the

water, they're exciting. They twist and turn. I caught a mako shark in Bimini, and it's in my studio in Palm Beach. I've got pictures of my Corvettes below it. That's where I got the impetus to do the [experimental] Manta Ray and those things.

"I just did those names . . . of mine—the fish names. They didn't like those, but we'd get them out anyway. Everything had to be a 'C.' I don't know how [Stingray] got to be that way; I meant it to be two words."

Opposite page, top: First-generation Corvettes were given impetus by Harley Earl (bottom). Top: Bill Mitchell was responsible for the Stingray racer (above), which led directly to the '63 Sting Ray.

Zora Arkus-Duntov: Mr. Corvette

Although many talented GM people have played a part in the Corvette's evolution, none has played a larger role than Zora Arkus-Duntov. Within the company and among the 'Vette's many millions of fans, he was known as "Mr. Corvette."

Duntov became involved with the Corvette relatively late in his professional career, at age 43. However, he had already achieved a measure of recognition before joining GM in May 1953. The Belgian-born engineer had worked as a technical consultant for Sydney Allard in England, where he developed the famous "Ardun" cylinder head conversion for the Ford/Mercury flathead V-8. After a stint with Fairchild Aviation, Duntov sent a copy of a research report that he had written on high-performance engines to Ed Cole, then head of Chevy engineering. On the basis of that report, Duntov was offered a position with GM Research and Development.

The Corvette was being launched about the time that Duntov arrived. Though he generally liked the car, he found that its handling left something to be desired, and he started fiddling with it on his own time. Not long afterward, management noticed his tinkering and began to give him regular Corvette assignments. The rest is history.

Duntov was not only an excellent engineer; he was also quite capable as a race driver. In 1956, for example, he and Betty Skelton drove modified Corvettes to better than 150 mph at the Daytona Speed Weeks. That also marked the birth of the so-called "Duntov cam" which boosted the popularity of Chevy's small-block V-8 among hot rodders in the Fifties. The following year he assisted with track-testing the futuristic Corvette SS racer at Sebring, although the effort failed due to an overly tight bushing which forced the car to be retired after only 23 laps.

Throughout his 25 years as chief Corvette engineer, Duntov approached his work with the energy of a much younger man. His accomplishments are many and important. He helped to develop Chevy's "Ramjet" fuel injection system, created the prototype for the aborted mid-engine Q-model Corvette, and designed the 1963 Sting Ray chassis, which remained in production basically unchanged for an unprecedented two decades. He retired from GM in late 1974.

About the Sting Ray: "[Work on the Sting Ray] began in '59, both chassis and engine. Before that, I was named Director of High Performance Vehicles. I took pride in the small-block Chevrolet engine. The whole car was good, though. Ergonomics were very good. It was quite adequate as an envelope, with such things as a shift lever location that would fall into the hand readily, good legibility of the gauges, and performance that was *non pareil* overall.

"[Sting Ray chassis design was] no problem; everything worked as designed. As testimony for that, the Sting Ray chassis. . .lasted up to the 1982 model. .

"[Bill Mitchell and I] were on the same wavelength. I only remember one disagreement—the split window on the '63 Sting Ray."

About the 1968 Corvette: "As a whole, design-wise, it was a very good car. Something got lost in the ergonomics, though. You had to move to operate the gearshift. The first thing I did was to provide more shoulder room. It was so pinched you couldn't drive it without leaning. To gain a half-inch per side I spent $120,000 retooling door inners. This half an inch was very significant.

"Another consideration: the '63–'67 car was a terrible 'lifter' aerodynamically. The subsequent design was also a lifter, but not to that extent."

David R. McLellan: The New Generation, Part I

David R. McLellan replaced Zora Arkus-Duntov as the head of Corvette engineering in 1975. He, too, is a unique personality, and the sixth-generation Corvette is the first to reflect it fully.

McLellan was born in the Upper Peninsula of Michigan in the mid-Thirties. His family then moved to Detroit, where McLellan grew up. He remained there for his college education at Wayne State University, where he majored in mechanical engineering. He went to GM in 1959, fresh out of school, and worked first at the corpora-tion's Milford proving grounds. He spent the better part of a decade there, during which he obtained a master's degree in engineering mechanics from Wayne State.

In 1968, McLellan was transferred to Chevrolet Division, where he worked on the second-generation Camaro. He was also involved with John DeLorean's proposal for a common chassis intended for the Camaro, the compact Nova, and possibly, he says, for the Corvette.

McLellan's next career step came in 1973—a year's sojourn at MIT as a Sloan Fellow sponsored by Chevrolet. The experience was an important one: It gave him the opportunity to learn first-hand about the automotive industry in other countries. He returned to Chevrolet in '74, and was given his first Corvette assignment as a staff engineer under Duntov. Just six months later, Duntov retired and McLellan was named chief Corvette engineer.

McLellan had clearly established himself as a clever and capable designer. He had to be: He had the formidable challenge of engineering and overseeing development of the first all-new Corvette in some 20 years.

About the sixth-generation Corvette: "As we analyzed the old car, a lot of things, we felt, were right. . . That was reflected in its performance in the market-place. We really look at this new Corvette as an ultimate perfor-mance statement by Chevrolet. With the old Corvette, we had kind of let things slip a little bit. We had not been pounding the table with our management as hard as we should have. We certainly are today.

"[The fifth-generation Corvette] had been updated year by year. It progressed dramatically in '81 and '82 when we moved production from St. Louis to Bowling Green. It was Jerry Palmer and the design team who worked closely together.

"I can't think of any great disagreements we had with Palmer. Once we laid down where the engine and people were, it was Jerry fine-tuning the design. I think Jerry was very satisfied with the design, and so were we."

Jerry Palmer: The New Generation, Part II

Since 1974, Jerry Palmer has been the head of Chevrolet's production Studio Three, where the sixth-generation Corvette took shape. More important, he has had overall responsibility for Corvette design since his redoubtable predecessor, William L. Mitchell, retired as GM's vice-president for design in 1977.

Palmer claims to be one of the few designers in the domestic industry who's a native Detroiter. His experience with GM Design goes all the way back to 1964, when he spent a summer in Design as a student. After graduating from the Center of Creative Studies in Detroit the following year, he joined GM permanently, completed the company's internship program, and then served briefly in the Advanced Studios at Design Staff. After a stint in the Army during 1966–67, he returned to Chevrolet and has been with that division ever since, except for brief assign-ments at GM subsidiaries in Europe and Japan. His first Corvette involvement came in 1969 when he assisted Bill Mitchell in creating several show models.

Jerry Palmer's affable, easy-going personality belies an intense enthusiasm for his work, about which he is uncharacteristically modest for such a high-ranking executive. He's always eager to talk Corvettes despite a hectic schedule.

About the sixth-generation Corvette roadster: "Right from the outset when we did the new car, there was always a roadster in the back of our mind. When we did the current car, back in the earlier sketches, you'd see sketches or renderings of roadsters. If we're talking about a true sports car, a top should be removed, more so than what we do with a targa top.

"We really didn't know that there was a shot at doing [the roadster] until Heinz Prechter [of American Sunroof] built a car up off of some early sketches, and we were involved on a very limited basis. But he took the bull by the

horns and built a Corvette conver-tible. And that's where the car came from. . . that's when the car became a very serious proposal. One drove up in front of the offices one day. Got everyone's attention. It was a. . . knock-out!

"The car lends itself very well to being a convertible. We knew that, and some of the sketches that we had done showed that. Probably the first thing that it smacks of, proportion-wise, is a Daytona roadster. It really emphasizes the rake of the windshield, because all of a sudden you have a notchback [with the roof up]. . . top up or down, you have a very striking car.

"We wanted to stay abreast with what our competition is doing. In fact, we want to lead the compe-tition.

"The [roadster] is so sophis-ticated in so many ways that I think some simplicity [in the manually operated cloth top] is needed to accent the technical achievements."

Opposite page: Zora Arkus-Duntov was the chief Corvette engineer for 25 years. Left: Dave McLellan is the present head of Corvette engineering. Above: Jerry Palmer heads Corvette design.

1986 Corvette Roadster

Corvette's Newest Roadster

The sixth generation of the Corvette was introduced for the 1984 model year, being lower, shorter, and lighter than it had been in 10 years. From nose to tail, the uniframe, drivetrain, and interior showed the results of engineering and styling working closely together, as discussed in Chapter 7.

Two systems that bear mentioning for 1986 are the Vehicle Anti-Theft System (VATS) and the computerized anti-lock braking system (ABS). Both are standard equipment. VATS is electronic, with sensors in the doors and hatch that trigger an alarm. Should a thief thwart the sensors, using the wrong key will render ignition impossible. Delays of up to half an hour could be faced by a thief in attempting to start the Corvette, and that length of time is too long for most of them to endure.

The anti-lock braking is based on the Bosch ABS II design. Computerized, the system acts to prevent the brakes from locking during panic stops, while at the same time making maximum use of the traction possible through each wheel. Sensors in each wheel determine when it is beginning to lock. The information from the sensors is monitored by the computerized control unit, which modulates the brake pressure hydraulically. The result is pulse-like control throughout the braking procedure that prevents loss of control due to skidding. Handling is improved also, with less effort needed to correct the steering of the car.

Another improvement since the introduction of the new Corvette is in its powerplant. The same engine that has powered all Corvettes since 1981 has returned for 1986—the 5.7-liter V-8. It utilizes the Bosch hotwire multipoint fuel

injection system which Chevrolet
introduced in 1985. New features
on the engine for '86 include
centrally located copper core spark
plugs, larger inlet ports, and
sintered metal valve seats.

Changes in the coupe version's
uniframe were necessary to produce Corvette convertibles with
appropriately rigid bodies. Birdcage
pieces have been reinforced, with
stronger braces and cross members,

The '86 roadster is powered by a
5.7-liter/350-cubic-inch V-8.

and added reinforcements were given to the uniframe. Door latches were strengthened. The top mechanism was made of aluminum in order to reduce its mass. Besides other subtle suspension and steering differences, the convertibles all have the 9.5-inch wheels of the coupe's Z51 Performance Handling Package, but the Z51 is not available in the convertible.

The 70th running of the Indianapolis 500 makes the Corvette roadster highly visible in 1986. In its yellow and black markings, the pace car is essentially stock—the first stock pace car since the last time that the Corvette led the championship cars around the 2½-mile oval for the May classic in 1978. In effect, all Corvette roadsters for 1986—no matter what their color—will be considered "pace cars." The application of the pace car graphics

shipped with each roadster will be at the discretion of the owner.

The roadster adds another chapter to the Corvette story. Some people would even argue that the roadster version of the car is the only true version.

Driving Impression

For the first time since 1975, Chevrolet has made its Corvette an honest sports car. After more than a decade's absence, the ragtop's

reintroduction brought with it a certain amount of apprehension. The Corvette of ten years ago was almost like a creature from another place and time compared to this one. How would the new roadster withstand the transition to the Corvette's new body style?

The scene was Yosemite National Park in late summer. Accepting an invitation to drive the new Corvette roadsters had been a matter of course, something about which little thought was allowed.

Opposite page: Stock Corvette pace cars for 1986 (above) and 1978 (below). Top: Driving impressions came from cruising Yosemite National Park in California. Above: Test cars flanked by a '75 roadster.

Yanking someone from behind a desk in the Midwest and expecting him to cope with California mountains behind the wheel of a Corvette roadster has to be somewhat akin to the radical changes faced by a baby first encountering the harsh realities beyond the womb.

Two groups of the make were lined up, waiting for their drivers and passengers. The dread of engine wheeze struck home—sustaining performance would be difficult. The tops were lowered, with only the side windows raised. That didn't last long, either—if the top's going to be lowered, so should the windows. A maxim for our time? Six of the Chevy ragtops stood in a row, all of them begging to be taken onto the road.

Opening the top of the Corvette distracts almost anyone's attention from the interior, either seating or instrumentation. They don't force themselves on you, providing a comfortable, supportive driving position that you can adjust quickly and an electronic dashboard that's the most visible in sunlight of all the electronic dashes available at this time. Controls for the mirrors and the seats were at hand, and once their locations were memorized, they were easily operated by touch. The body-mounted shift lever was a quick motion of the right hand away from the steering wheel. Shifts had a mechanical feel—not liquid or fluid like a Volvo, but not as vague as some of the cable-actuated linkages, either.

The first group of cars encountered all had manual transmissions. Nothing wheezy could be attributed to the performance of the Corvette roadsters, although the Chevrolet engineers assured the drivers that the cars wouldn't run as well at 8000 feet as they would in the Arizona desert. So be it. Shifting into gear at the start of the trek through the winding mountain roads was fairly comfortable, as the clutch felt substantial without demanding the use of overwhelming pressure. It wasn't as awkward to use as those in some of the more recent pony cars. Another aspect of the 'Vette that feels good is the sense of space from the cockpit to the front bumper.

The rise in the fenders isn't

CORVETTE ROADSTER SPECIFICATIONS

Generation	First	Second	Third	Fourth	Fifth	Sixth
Model Years	1953–55	1956–57	1958–62	1963–67	1968–75	1986–
Production	4640	9806	54,569	72,418	70,583	Est. 6000 (1986)
Base Price	$2799–3523	$3149–3465	$3631–4038	$4037–4141	$4141–6550	Est. $30,000
Dimensions and Capacities						
Wheelbase (in.):	102.0	102.0	102.0	98.0	98.0	96.0
Length (in.):	167.0	168.0	177.2	175.2	182.5–185.5	176.5
Width (in.):	72.2	70.5	72.8	69.2	69.0	71.0
Height (in.):	52.1	52.0	52.4	49.6	47.8–48.0	46.9
Front Track (in.):	57.0	57.0	57.0	56.8	58.7	59.4
Rear Track (in.):	59.0	59.0	59.0	57.6	59.4–59.5	60.4
Curb Weight (lb.):	2705	2880	3080	3130	3280–3530	Est. 3150
Performance						
Selected 0–60 mph (sec):	8.8	5.8	5.9	5.5	5.9	Est. 6.0
Selected Top Speed (mph):	118	133	132	143	150	150

'86 Corvette—70th Indy 500 pace car.

so overwhelming that you think you're driving a slingshot rail.

Little time was given to familiarization before reaching touring speed on the twisting and hilly terrain. But the Corvette is forgiving enough for you to jump in and go without a great deal of preparation. While on the one hand you know that enough horsepower lies underfoot, you also understand that abuse of that power will put you into dire straits. The car is forgiving and tractable enough for running around town, but it's also strong enough to get you into trouble if not respected.

Thinking of being able to "throw around" a 3100-pound automobile brings to mind some amusing images, but after a while—after encountering never-ending sequences of turns—you have the feeling that the roadster is capable of some nimble maneuverings—a far cry from the more ponderous offerings of the past. Still, the new roadster has the nimbleness of a tiger rather than that of a cheetah. Its cat-like feet not only corner with assurance, holding the car's body flat in combination with its suspension, but works in conjunction with the new anti-lock braking system (ABS) to pull down the speed of the auto without sliding. Finding a clear stretch of highway to the rear took some doing, but slamming the brake pedal as close to the floorboard as possible made the wait worthwhile. No skidding resulted from the overambitious braking maneuver, although some slight steering corrections were necessary.

With more than adequate acceleration, tires and wheels suited to the handling needs of most drivers, a visually and physically supportive interior, the roadster has a suspension that's taut, but certainly livable for long distances.

So pull out the small suitcases and pack up the most tightly foldable clothes from the closet. The time has come for some open-air fun. Put down the top, and head for the warm weather. A few thousand miles in the Corvette roadster will probably leave you yearning for even more.

CORVETTE ROADSTER ENGINES

Type	Cubic-Inch Displ.	Comp. Ratio (:1)	Fuel Delivery	Brake Horsepower @ RPM (SAE gross)
First Generation (1953–55)				
OHV I-6	235.5	8.0	Carburetor	150 @ 4200
				155 @ 4200
OHV V-8	265.0	8.0	Carburetor	195 @ 5000
Second Generation (1956–57)				
OHV V-8	265.0	9.25	Carburetor	210 @ 5200
				225 @ 5200
OHV V-8	283.0	9.5	Carburetor	220 @ 4800
				245 @ 5000
		10.5	Fuel Injection	283 @ 6200
Third Generation (1958–62)				
OHV V-8	283.0	9.5	Carburetor	230 @ 4800
				245 @ 5000
			Fuel Injection	250 @ 5000
			Carburetor	270 @ 6000
		10.5	Fuel Injection	290 @ 6200
		11.0		275 @ 5200
				315 @ 6200
OHV V-8	327.0	10.5	Carburetor	250 @ 4400
				300 @ 5000
		11.25		340 @ 6000
			Fuel Injection	360 @ 6000
Fourth Generation (1963–67)				
OHV V-8	327.0	10.5	Carburetor	250 @ 4400
				300 @ 5000
		11.25		340 @ 6000
			Fuel Injection	360 @ 6000
			Carburetor	365 @ 6200
			Fuel Injection	375 @ 6200
		11.0	Carburetor	350 @ 5800
OHV V-8	396.0	11.0	Carburetor	425 @ 6400
OHV V-8	427.0	10.25	Carburetor	390 @ 5400
		11.0		425 @ 6400
Fifth Generation (1968–75)				
OHV V-8	327.0	10.5	Carburetor	300 @ 5000
		11.0		350 @ 5800
OHV V-8	350.0	10.25	Carburetor	300 @ 4800
		11.0		350 @ 5600
				370 @ 6000 (1)
		8.5		270 @ 4800
		9.0		330 @ 5600 (2)
		8.5		195 @ 4400*
		9.0		250 @ 5200*
		8.5		165 @ 3800*
		9.0		205 @ 4800*
OHV V-8	427.0	10.25	Carburetor	390 @ 5400
		10.25		400 @ 5400
		11.0		435 @ 5800
		12.5		430 @ 5200 (3)
OHV V-8	454.0	10.25	Carburetor	390 @ 4800
		12.25		465 @ 5200 (4)
		8.5		365 @ 4800
		9.0		425 @ 5600 (5)
				270 @ 4400
Sixth Generation (1986)				
OHV V-8	350.0	9.5	Fuel Injection	230 @ 4000*

(1) LT-1, 1970; (2) LT-1, 1971-72; (3) L-88, 1969; (4) LS-7, 1970; (5) LS-6, 1972; *SAE net horsepower